MW01148709

FACES AND PLACES
OF IUPUI

WELL HOUSE
BOOKS

FACES AND PLACES OF IUPUI

Fifty Years in Indianapolis

Cassidy Hunter and **Becky Wood**

Foreword by **Nasser H. Paydar**
Introduction by **James T. Morris**
Epilogue by **Olivia Pretorius**

INDIANA UNIVERSITY PRESS

This book is a publication of

Indiana University Press
Office of Scholarly Publishing
Herman B Wells Library 350
1320 East 10th Street
Bloomington, Indiana 47405 USA

indiana.org

Manufactured in the United States of America

ISBN 978-0-253-05153-0 (cloth)
ISBN 978-0-253-05156-1 (ebook)

First printing 2020

CONTENTS

Foreword

Nasser H. Paydar
Chancellor of IUPUI and Executive
Vice President of Indiana University

THE FIRST TIME I STEPPED foot on the IUPUI campus as a young faculty member in 1985, I never expected that I would later find myself serving as chancellor of this very campus more than three decades later as we celebrated its 50th anniversary. In all these years, I have seen the campus grow and change in ways impossible to imagine. Over time, one might expect a campus like ours to grow in terms of the number of faculty, staff, students, and buildings, but at IUPUI we constantly push ourselves beyond the expected. That explains why we are home to the world's first motorsports engineering program and why scholars here today are at the cutting edge in designing technology for autonomous vehicles. It's why we're home to the world's first and most respected school of philanthropy. It's why we discovered the cure for testicular cancer. These are all part of the history of IUPUI.

Faces and Places of IUPUI: Fifty Years in Indianapolis captures the collaborative spirit that has constantly reshaped our campus, pushing it toward innovation for the past half century. From the very beginning, this collection was driven by the campus community, with faculty, staff, and students nominating and then voting on the people they considered to be "Faces of IUPUI." Profiles of the Faces of IUPUI appeared on social media and on the 50th Anniversary website throughout the year, with a culminating exhibition in the Cultural Arts Gallery at the IUPUI Campus Center. I feel humbled to be included among these Faces of IUPUI, considering the many distinguished people who have contributed so much to shaping this campus.

These stories encourage and inspire. So many of these Faces of IUPUI have returned to this campus again and again, studying here as students and coming back as faculty and staff members. In my case, I started my career here; was then selected as the vice chancellor and dean of what was then called the IUPUI Center in Columbus, Indiana; and went on to serve as the chancellor at IU East in Richmond, Indiana. Like other Jaguars, I returned, drawn back by the qualities that distinguish IUPUI from every other university in the country. And like those others, I know this campus and love it. This place draws people in and does not let them go.

The landscape of the campus has also evolved to meet the changing needs of our faculty, staff, and students. You will see some of those changes represented in the pages that follow, including the construction of Wood Fountain and the Campus Center, two IUPUI landmarks. You will be able to trace the highlights of IUPUI's 50th Anniversary year, including Jagathon, IUPUI's Dance Marathon; the IUPUI Regatta; and the Birthday Bash. And you will read about the growth of the campus over the course of our first fifty years.

Of course, this growth is not just physical. Just as IUPUI's footprint has expanded, so have our academic programs. As the most comprehensive university campus in the state, IUPUI offers Indiana University as well as Purdue University degrees. A national leader in the health and life sciences, IUPUI is home to the only dental school in the state and one of the largest schools of nursing in the country. In addition, it offers a wide array of professional degrees, including law, engineering, business, and education, to name just a few. This and so much more give IUPUI a great deal to celebrate.

As chancellor of IUPUI, I am pleased to present and endorse *Faces and Places of IUPUI: Fifty Years in Indianapolis*, which may be considered a people's history of our campus. It chronicles IUPUI's first fifty years and tells our campus's unique story in a way it has never been told before. It also captures the tremendous energy of the IUPUI campus. Each element in this collection adds a new dimension to IUPUI's story as it has grown into a national and international leader in education and research, and each one reminds me why I love this campus and its people.

Acknowledgments

Cassidy Hunter

THE FACES OF IUPUI CAMPAIGN was one of my first projects when I moved into my role as communications specialist in the Office of the Chancellor at IUPUI, and it is one I am tremendously honored to have helped lead. I have been humbled and touched by the overwhelmingly positive response to the Faces of IUPUI campaign by those who were profiled, by those who participated in the nomination and selection process, and by our readers.

I would like to extend a special thanks to Becky Wood, communications director in the Office of the Chancellor and my coauthor, for her thoughtful guidance and encouragement every step of the way. And my sincere gratitude goes to Milana Katic, multimedia communications specialist in the Office of the Chancellor, who served as the project manager for Faces of IUPUI. Without her organizational expertise and personal support, I am certain this campaign would not have been elevated to award-winning status.

My appreciation and heartfelt thanks go out to the students, staff and faculty members, alumni, and community partners who served as the Faces of IUPUI. Each of them generously gave of their time and shared incredibly personal memories and stories with me about their experience at and with IUPUI and its impact on them. Each profile left me feeling prouder than the one before—proud of all that these Jaguars have achieved, not just for themselves but for us all.

A final note of thanks to my sweet family, especially my husband Adam and my son Caleb, who are my biggest cheerleaders each and every day, no matter the cause.

Becky Wood

THE FACES AND PLACES OF IUPUI PROJECT—from its initial conceptualization to its transformation into this volume—represents the remarkably collaborative spirit of IUPUI. Faculty, staff, students, and members of the community came together to nominate, select, and celebrate these Faces of IUPUI. This campaign and the resulting volume have achieved a number of 50th Anniversary goals, including recognizing the history of our campus and those who have helped build it over the years as well as strengthening pride in the IUPUI community.

Thousands of people engaged with the Faces profiles on the 50th Anniversary website, Twitter, Instagram, and Facebook every week as new Faces were unveiled. Abdullah Alzeer even ended up on a Saudi Arabian national news program due to his being named a Face of IUPUI. Other Faces were featured in their hometown newspapers. Being a Face of IUPUI has become a point of pride for those receiving this recognition.

It was my honor to lead the 50th Anniversary Communications Committee and to be part of the Faces of IUPUI campaign, which led to this volume. I want to extend my sincere gratitude to a number of people without whom this volume would not exist. Chancellor Nasser Paydar encouraged the campus to achieve what he called "big impact with a wow factor" during the anniversary year and gave faculty, staff, and students the freedom to shape this celebration into one that we would all remember. In addition, Cassidy Hunter, communications specialist in the Office of the Chancellor, deserves special commendation for writing all the Faces of IUPUI profiles that are included in this volume. She did yeoman's work on research and interviews. Without her dedication and skill, this project would have been well-nigh impossible. Milana Katic, multimedia communications specialist in the chancellor's office, was the project manager of Faces of IUPUI, notifying our honorees, keeping our editorial calendar, locating photographs, creating web pages, promoting Faces of IUPUI on social media, and much more. As with Cassidy, without Milana, the Faces project would likely be on the cutting-room floor right now.

I wish I could mention every other person across campus and beyond who had a hand in pulling together this material and sharing it over the past year, but an exhaustive list would also be an exhausting one. I would, however, like to thank the members of the 50th Anniversary Communications Committee and especially the Digital Strategy Subcommittee. I also want to give special thanks to those in IUPUI Special Collections and Archives, who provided historic photographs. A final set of thanks goes to the team in IU Studios and especially photographer Liz Kaye, whose great skill is in evidence throughout this volume.

I would also like to offer an official word of thanks to the IU Bicentennial Committee that approved this volume as part of the Publication and Media Series. I am grateful to Gary Dunham, director of IU Press, who guided and supported our efforts.

This acknowledgement would not be complete without two final notes of thanks. To Christine Fitzpatrick, director of the 50th Anniversary celebration and former chief of staff to the chancellor: You are the best kind of colleague and friend—one who quietly and with confidence makes us all feel that together, we can honor the great history of our campus, recognize the people who shaped it, and do so in ways that create lasting legacies and traditions that reinforce the values we share: service, integrity, diversity, and inclusion, as well as academic excellence. Without your leadership and vision, this magnificent year of celebration would have been much less in every respect. Without you, this volume might not have been even imagined, much less written.

And to my husband, Will: You have my endless gratitude and love, though not necessarily in that order.

FACES AND PLACES
OF IUPUI

Introduction

James T. Morris
Vice Chairman of Pacers Sports and Entertainment and Indiana University Trustee

JANUARY 24, 2019, WAS ONE of the most exciting days in the history of Indianapolis, the state of Indiana, and Indiana and Purdue universities. We celebrated the fiftieth birthday and anniversary of IUPUI.

At the celebration, Indiana University President Michael A. McRobbie, IUPUI Chancellor Nasser H. Paydar, and Purdue University Trustee Chair Michael Berghoff made inspiring, uplifting, and optimistic statements about the future of IUPUI. Each of the five extraordinary living mayors of Indianapolis talked about the history of IUPUI and their role in developing this remarkable, exciting experiment in higher education. Richard Lugar, Stephen Goldsmith, Bart Peterson, Greg Ballard, and Joe Hogsett all participated, and the spirit of the late Bill Hudnut, mayor of Indianapolis from 1976 to 1992, was very much alive in the room. The fact that Senator Lugar passed away only a few months after this event adds special meaning to his presence at IUPUI that day. *Inside Indiana Business* host Gerry Dick moderated the event. Seeing several thousand students participating in the celebration, so excited and enthusiastic about their university, made the morning extra special.

Some of the extraordinary statistics shared that day tell the story of IUPUI. Since 1969, IUPUI has graduated 210,528 students. Those students have come from every county in Indiana, every state in the nation, and 144 different countries. And more good news is that a large percentage of these graduates stay in Indiana to build their careers. Today, IUPUI employs 8,131 people on the faculty and staff. This payroll, plus goods and services purchased by the campus, contribute more than \$1 billion annually to our local economy.

In addition, \$7.7 billion in research has taken place on the campus since 1969. The university offers 478 separate degree programs and more than 8,000 different courses, has one of the most impressive distance-education programs of any university in the country, and, in 2019, the campus graduated 7,021 students.

These numbers are remarkable by any measurement. Twenty-eight percent of the students at IUPUI represent minority populations. IUPUI is home to the largest medical school in the United States; our schools of nursing and dentistry are also among the largest in the country; and the Lilly Family School of Philanthropy is the single most important academic center studying philanthropy. The School of Social Work is more than one hundred years old, and the McKinney School of Law, Fairbanks School of Public Health, and School of Informatics and Computing are preparing next-generation professionals in key areas, including STEM fields. And I would be remiss if I failed to mention the extraordinary Herron School of Art and Design, which features some of IUPUI's most creative programs. Today, enrollment at IUPUI is nearly 30,000 students.

To think about what all of this means to the future of our city and state is exciting, powerful, and a bit overwhelming. In 2017, IUPUI joined the Horizon League for athletics, and in 2017–2018, the Natatorium hosted thirty-seven competitive events enjoyed by 147,285 visitors. The campus is magnificent, is superbly located in the heart of our state's capital, and now has considerable residential facilities for its students.

IUPUI is innovative, collaborative, and highly resourceful. I am proud of the leadership of Indiana and Purdue universities and the incredible individuals who should feel great pride and satisfaction in what they have built. IUPUI will make a critical contribution to our city and state's future. Truly, it is a blessing and worthy of the support of every single Hoosier.

Great universities educate, serve their communities, advance knowledge through research, and generally prepare their students for happy, productive, caring, and serving lives and to become thoughtful parents, leaders, and citizens. IUPUI has had this impact and more on all of us.

This volume comes at a particularly important time for Indiana University as it celebrates its first two hundred years of providing outstanding education and conducting research that changes our world. IUPUI's first fifty years add to the richness of the university as a whole, and its anniversary celebration serves as a launching pad for the IU Bicentennial.

As a trustee of Indiana University, a great friend of the IUPUI campus, and a proud citizen of Indianapolis, I would like to offer my gratitude to the five extraordinary leaders who have served as chancellors of IUPUI. Maynard Hine and Glenn Irwin laid the foundation upon which Gerald Bepko and Charles Bantz continued to build, and now Nasser Paydar is providing powerful and visionary leadership, working in partnership with the city. All of their stories and many others appear in the following pages where you will also find fifty years of impressive impact, outstanding collaborations, and remarkable Jaguar spirit.

As Richard Lugar once said, "Every great city needs a great university," and I would add the good news that Indianapolis now has one in IUPUI.

Spotlight on IUPUI History

The IUPUI campus begins to take shape
with the construction of Cavanaugh Hall

1. AFFIRMING OUR PAST
The Campus Takes Shape

THOUGH IUPUI CELEBRATED ITS 50TH ANNIVERSARY year in 2019, the history of the campus dates back nearly to the turn of the twentieth century, with the establishment of the Indiana University School of Medicine in 1903. A population center in the state of Indiana, Indianapolis provided a fertile training ground for doctors, dentists, nurses, and other health care professionals, and IU capitalized on this, developing a comprehensive urban campus with a special emphasis on the health professions. Midway through the twentieth century, Purdue University began offering technical programs in Indianapolis on its 38th Street campus near the Indiana State Fairgrounds. In 1969, with the endorsement and leadership of then-Mayor of Indianapolis Richard G. Lugar, IU and Purdue University agreed to establish IUPUI as the campus home for both IU and Purdue academic programs under the management and oversight of the IU administration. The Faces of IUPUI that follow reflect the earliest days of IUPUI as a campus.

Facing View of the west side of Cavanaugh Hall during construction, circa 1970. *Photo courtesy of IUPUI Special Collections and Archives (UA24–003576).*

Above Cavanaugh Hall groundbreaking on September 4, 1968, with IU Chancellor and Interim President Herman B Wells, Dean of IU Downtown Campus in Indianapolis Joseph T. Taylor, then-Mayor of Indianapolis Richard Lugar, IU Trustee Donald C. Danielson, and outgoing IU President Elvis J. Stahr Jr. *Photo courtesy of IUPUI Special Collections and Archives (UA24–003579).*

Maynard K. Hine as a young man (undated). *Photo courtesy of IUPUI Special Collections and Archives (UA024_006752).*

Maynard K. Hine

First Chancellor of IUPUI (1969–1973);
Dean Emeritus of the IU School of Dentistry

WELL BEFORE HE HELPED LEAD EFFORTS to create an urban university called IUPUI, Dr. Maynard K. Hine was already helping his fellow Hoosiers. A native Hoosier himself, Hine joined the Indiana University School of Dentistry in Indianapolis in 1944 and became dean the following year. Under his twenty-five-year leadership, the state's only dental school saw incredible growth in enrollment and developed a reputation for outstanding academic and research programs. Hine's collaborative spirit brought him together with other key university, city, and state leaders in 1968 to lay the groundwork for IUPUI.

"Chancellor Hine left behind a legacy of leadership on our campus," said IUPUI's fifth chancellor, Nasser H. Paydar. "He served as chancellor from 1969 to 1973 and oversaw a period of tremendous growth and change for IUPUI. In addition to increasing enrollment and credit hours, he led our campus from being a loose collection of schools and programs to being a more unified institution. This growth suggests Chancellor Hine's powerful legacy."

That legacy continues at IUPUI. Hine Hall was named for and dedicated in Hine's honor in early 2013. Two of Hine's grandsons are also IU-trained dentists, one of whom—Dr. William Hine—is on the faculty of the IU School of Dentistry.

"From every story I have been told and my observations growing up, my grandfather had a love for this campus and a passion for academics," said Maynard Hine's grandson William Hine.

In addition to his distinguished campus leadership, Chancellor Hine was an innovative pioneer in dental education and was renowned in the field. His impact was far-reaching, from lending his expertise to several professional organizations to coauthoring five books and receiving countless awards that honor his vast accomplishments.

"Dr. Hine's contributions to the campus, to the city of Indianapolis, and to higher education were enormous," said IU President Michael A. McRobbie. "He served as chancellor during the important formative years of IUPUI. His visionary leadership contributed to the foundation that has enabled IUPUI to become one of the premier urban research campuses in the nation."

Hine passed away in 1996.

Above Then-Dean of the School of Dentistry Hine and Indiana University President Herman B Wells personally check out the equipment for the 1958 groundbreaking for the addition to the dental school. *Photo courtesy of IUPUI Special Collections and Archives (UA024_006883).*

Facing From left: IUPUI's first three chancellors—Gerald L. Bepko, Glenn W. Irwin Jr., and Maynard K. Hine—in 1989. *Photo courtesy of IUPUI Special Collections and Archives (UA24–002573).*

Joseph T. Taylor
Founding Dean of the School of Liberal Arts at IUPUI; Professor of Sociology

DR. JOSEPH T. TAYLOR, THE FIRST DEAN of IUPUI's School of Liberal Arts, was an integral partner in the creation of the IUPUI campus in 1969. Indiana University President Herman B Wells had tapped him to play this pivotal role because of Taylor's unique ability to build consensus, effectively manage relationships, and positively influence people, a collaborative approach that became a model for IUPUI in its growing role within Indianapolis.

Taylor grew up in the Jim Crow South, attending the historically black Wiley College in Marshall, Texas. He transferred to the University of Illinois where he received his bachelor's and master's degrees. Taylor's doctoral studies at IU were interrupted in 1942 when he was deployed with the US Army to Europe until 1945. Soon after he left the military, Taylor married Hertha Mae Ward, an educator who spent her career teaching in the Indianapolis Public Schools system.

In 1957, prior to IUPUI's official creation, the Taylors moved to Indianapolis, and Joseph Taylor joined IU in 1962 as an associate professor of sociology. He served as dean of the IU Downtown Campus in Indianapolis from 1967 to 1970 and was the first dean of the School of Liberal Arts at IUPUI, a position he held until 1978. After retiring as dean, Taylor continued to teach and serve as a special assistant to campus leaders until he was named professor emeritus in 1983.

"As an African American, Dr. Taylor was a pioneer at every stage of his academic career," said Chancellor Emeritus Charles R. Bantz. "He infused that perseverance and ability to break new ground into the very core of what has made IUPUI successful today."

Deeply committed to the Indianapolis community, Taylor didn't limit his impact to campus. He played a key role in the integration of Indianapolis Public Schools, serving as one of two commissioners who assisted school officials in the desegregation effort.

When the School of Liberal Arts created a symposium focused on issues related to urban life and diversity, leaders chose to recognize Taylor by naming the event in his honor. The Joseph T. Taylor Symposium celebrated its thirtieth year in 2019 and takes place each spring. The building that houses University College, one of the cornerstones of undergraduate students' academic lives at IUPUI, was renamed Joseph T. Taylor Hall in 2011.

Taylor passed away in 2000.

Right Former Dean of the IU Downtown Campus and future Dean of the School of Liberal Arts Joseph T. Taylor works at his desk in 1971. *Photo courtesy of IUPUI Special Collections and Archives (UA24–008669).*

Below Dean Taylor at the School of Nursing Symposium in 1970 with Chancellor Irwin, Assistant Dean of the School of Nursing Frances Orgain, and Chancellor Emeritus Hine. *Photo courtesy of IUPUI Special Collections and Archives (UA024_006838).*

Glenn W. Irwin Jr.

Second Chancellor of IUPUI (1973–1986); Dean Emeritus of the IU School of Medicine

Dr. Glenn W. Irwin Jr. was appointed IUPUI's second chancellor in 1973, but his connection to Indiana University dates back much further. Revered and respected for his kindhearted nature, Irwin graduated from the IU School of Medicine in the spring of 1944, one of two wartime classes that year, the result of the school's push to produce more doctors to serve the injured troops.

After an internship at Methodist Hospital and a partial residency at the IU Medical Center, both in Indianapolis, he served in the US Army Medical Corps before returning to finish his residency at the IU Medical Center. Irwin joined the School of Medicine's faculty in 1950 and became its dean in 1965. Four years later, he was present when the Indianapolis extensions of IU and Purdue University merged to become IUPUI.

During his deanship, Irwin's focus on medical education resulted in the development of the "Indiana Plan" in the 1960s, the first comprehensive medical education program of its kind. This plan established seven additional campuses where the first two years of medical education were taught in collaboration with the science faculty. In 2012, in an effort to address physician shortages in underserved areas and to serve an aging population, the School of Medicine expanded the statewide system created by Irwin by adding third- and fourth-year options to those campuses.

Under Irwin's leadership as chancellor, IUPUI experienced a dramatic physical transformation and significant growth in every aspect of the university. Enrollment grew 35 percent to more than 23,000 students; full-time faculty increased from about 800 to more than 1,300; sponsored research increased from $21 million to nearly $41 million; and $200 million in new construction was completed, including the Business/School of Public and Environmental Affairs Building, the School of Law Building, the iconic IU Natatorium, and what is now the Michael A. Carroll Track and Soccer Stadium. Riley Hospital for Children and IU Hospital were each expanded, and both the Regenstrief Institute and the Ronald McDonald House were opened.

After Irwin retired in 1986, he maintained his connection to IUPUI and his office in the medical school for decades. IUPUI established the Glenn W. Irwin Jr., MD, Experience Excellence Award and the Glenn W. Irwin Jr., MD, Research Scholar Award in his honor.

"Glenn Irwin deepened IUPUI's connections with the community in its critical early years and remained dedicated to the success of the campus nearly a quarter century

Left Chancellor Irwin and Dean Emeritus of the Kelley School of Business Schuyler Otteson examine an artist's rendering of the proposed site of the new Business/School of Public and Environmental Affairs Building. *Photo courtesy of IUPUI Special Collections and Archives (UA024_002578).*

Right Glenn W. Irwin Jr. with medical records, circa 1950. *Photo courtesy of IUPUI Special Collections and Archives (UA24–000583).*

after having retired as chancellor," said Chancellor Emeritus Charles R. Bantz. "He faithfully attended key IUPUI events, including the annual Employee Recognition Ceremony and the Chancellor's Honors Convocation at which the excellence awards named for him are given."

Irwin continued to serve the Indianapolis community as a board member of the Eiteljorg Museum of American Indians and Western Art, the YMCA of Greater Indianapolis, and the Riley Children's Foundation.

Irwin passed away in 2012.

Linda Durr
Administrative Assistant, Office of Planning and Institutional Improvement

ON THE SAME DAY IN SEPTEMBER 1973 that Dr. Glenn W. Irwin Jr. became IUPUI's second chancellor, Linda Durr walked into her new career in the Office of the Vice Chancellor for Academic Affairs and Dean of the Faculties. Nearly five decades later, Durr still calls IUPUI home.

Now an administrative assistant in the Office of Planning and Institutional Improvement, Durr has witnessed IUPUI's growth and transformation firsthand for more than forty-five years, from her first office in the Union Building between Michigan and 10th Streets—a converted dry cleaner and now a parking lot—to her current location in University Hall, which was completed in 2015.

"I suppose I represent the hard-working staff members operating behind the scenes, providing important support to the leaders of the university," explained Durr of her role. "It has been a joy and a privilege to share in and be a small part of the growth of IUPUI. I have always been proud to introduce myself by saying, 'I work at IUPUI.'"

After twelve years in the Office of Academic Affairs, Durr decided to take some time off to spend with her daughter. Eighteen months later, Durr returned to IUPUI and a part-time role in the Office of the Associate Dean of the Faculties. In the summer of 1992, she joined the Office of Planning and Institutional Improvement under Vice Chancellor Trudy W. Banta, whom she assisted for twenty-four years until Banta's retirement in 2016.

"Linda's intelligence, cheerfulness, and commitment inspired me every day during all the years she and I worked together," Banta said. "It was that always-positive outlook and genuine caring for coworkers that helped to achieve zero turnover among our office staff for more than twenty years. I count Linda as the single most important source of support for whatever successes I achieved in my career at IUPUI."

A recipient of the Glenn W. Irwin Jr., MD, Experience Excellence Award in 1998 for her outstanding service to IUPUI, Durr is a well-known and widely respected member of the university staff. She is highly regarded among senior leadership on campus and among IUPUI partners in the community. Her warmth and graciousness embody IUPUI's welcoming campus.

Facing Linda Durr. *Photo by Liz Kaye / Indiana University.*

Stephen Hundley, senior advisor to the chancellor for planning and institutional improvement, said, "Everyone loves Linda. I consistently receive very positive feedback from all who interact with Linda about her professionalism, attention to detail, and willingness to go above and beyond her call of duty."

After all this time, Durr finds herself more challenged and more fulfilled in her role than ever before. "Fulfillment is difficult to define and achieve, but once you find fulfillment in your life, you become a happy, confident, and forward-thinking employee, friend, and family member," she said. "In effect, this is what IUPUI promised me some forty-five years ago—the possibility of 'fulfilling the promise' through challenging and important work assignments. I am a stronger and more focused person because of my IUPUI experience."

Facing top Linda Durr (left) with her former colleague Shirley Nusbaum in 1980. *Photo courtesy of Linda Durr.*

Facing bottom Durr with her former boss and IUPUI Vice Chancellor for Academic Affairs John C. Buhner; his wife, Betty; and Nusbaum at an event in the early 1990s. *Photo courtesy of Linda Durr.*

Diane Billings
Chancellor's Professor Emerita, IU School of Nursing

Retired Chancellor's Professor Emerita Diane Billings started her journey to becoming a Face of IUPUI in 1969. She began her teaching career as a faculty member in the Purdue University Associate Degree Program in Nursing at the 38th Street campus before the program became part of the IU School of Nursing on the downtown campus. A faculty member for nearly four decades until her retirement in 2006, Billings left an indelible mark on the School of Nursing, the IUPUI campus, and the field of nursing itself.

During her career, Billings taught courses in each of the school's academic programs. She also ensured that the School of Nursing retained its competitive edge in the age of digital and online learning by implementing a plan to put a computer on the

Diane Billings works at a computer in the 1980s. *Photo courtesy of the IU School of Nursing.*

desk of each faculty and staff member and developing a state-of-the-art computer lab for students in the early 1990s. An expert in distance education, Billings successfully applied for a Fund for the Improvement of Postsecondary Education grant for the development of three online academic courses designed specifically for critical care nurses. She then worked with a team to plan and develop each course.

Billings (right) with her former mentee Pamela Jeffries, who is now the dean of George Washington University School of Nursing. *Photo courtesy of the IU School of Nursing.*

In addition to her presence in the classroom, Billings also served as the associate dean of teaching, learning, and information resources. She oversaw the School of Nursing's Office of Lifelong Learning, Center for Excellence in Teaching, and computer cluster. Billings's legacy is visible today at the Simulation Center and the Learning Lab, which reflect the innovative technologies to which IUPUI students now have access thanks to her efforts.

"My career was propelled by a vision of excellence in teaching," said Billings. "Think big and realize that change is good. Find people who have the same mission and vision as you do and join forces to achieve your goal."

Billings has been honored with numerous awards for her work in nursing education. In 2002, she received the Ross Pioneer Spirit Award from the American Association of Critical-Care Nurses, and in 1999, she received the Sigma Theta Tau International Founders Award for Excellence in Teaching. She is a fellow of the American Academy of Nursing and received the organization's highest honor of Living Legend for her work in advancing the science of nursing education. Her book *Teaching in Nursing: A Guide for Faculty* won the American Journal of Nursing Book of the Year Award in 1998 and again in 2016.

In 2015, Billings, along with her husband, Richard, was awarded the IUPUI Spirit of Philanthropy Award, and in 2016, she received the President's Circle Laurel Pin, both commemorating her dedication to philanthropy. She has continued this commitment through gifts to the Emily Holmquist Lectureship, the Schweer Continuing Education Lectures, the McBride Professorship, the School of Nursing Faculty Award for Research in Nursing Education, and the Bepko Scholars and Fellows Program.

Virginia Harrison
IUPUI Class of 1972 and 1977, School of Education

Virginia Harrison and IUPUI have something special in common: They share a January 24 birthday. Harrison was born in 1949; twenty years later, Indiana University, Purdue University, and Indianapolis officials fulfilled a vision for the city and created IUPUI. But Harrison's connection to IUPUI runs deeper: She is also a two-time IUPUI graduate. Just months before the campus was officially established, a then-twenty-year-old Harrison applied to IU to study education at what was then called the IU Extension Center in Indianapolis.

At the time of Harrison's application, classes were held at extension sites in a variety of locations around the city, and this translated into a regular commute to 902 New York Street for evening classes after working her full-time job at an insurance company. As she worked toward her degree, she watched the campus take shape. Harrison, who earned her undergraduate degree in elementary education in 1972, was among the first School of Education students to start and finish their degree in Indianapolis.

"It has been exciting to watch the campus grow over the years, and especially to watch the School of Education grow to focus on urban education in our community," Harrison said.

She began teaching shortly after her graduation from IUPUI and devoted her teaching career to the school system that provided her foundation, Indianapolis Public Schools, where she was an educator for more than thirty years. Harrison returned to IUPUI and earned her master's degree in 1977.

"My entire teaching career was spent in Indianapolis Public Schools where I taught elementary education until I retired in 2004. During that time, I explored alternative teaching practices like Montessori and introduced subjects like economics and environmental education into my classroom," said Harrison.

Harrison served on the School of Education Alumni Board from 2005 to 2007, and her legacy continues at IUPUI where her daughter is currently a staff member.

"IUPUI has been and always will be my university," said Harrison.

Above Virginia Harrison chats with the School of Education's director of the Curriculum Resource Center, Erin Cassity, after learning they share many connections from the early days of the School of Education at IUPUI. *Photo by Liz Kaye / Indiana University.*

Facing Harrison holds a picture of herself from when she was a student at IUPUI. *Photo by Liz Kaye / Indiana University.*

Claudia Dille
IUPUI Class of 1978, School of Nursing

WITH TIES TO IUPUI DATING BACK TO 1970, School of Nursing alumna Claudia Dille, MSN, coupled her love of science and her desire to give back to the community to create a distinguished career as a nurse, educator, mentor, and advocate. That year, she came to Indiana to work at IU Hospital after completing her nursing undergraduate degree at Texas Woman's University in 1969.

Dille, who was still considering her long-term professional path, decided to pursue her master's degree in medical-surgical nursing at IUPUI with minors in teacher education and continuing education. During her graduate studies, she worked as a surgical intensive care unit staff nurse at IU Hospital. She also served as a resident lecturer in the Associate of Arts Degree in Nursing Program where she supervised and evaluated clinical assignments and participated in curriculum development.

After she graduated from IUPUI in 1978, Dille joined the Surgical and Adult Critical Care Nursing Services Division at the IU Medical Center where she stayed until 1995. Initially working as a staff development coordinator, she later became assistant to the associate director and eventually acting associate director. During her tenure, Dille led the planning, development, and implementation of the Continuing Education Program for Nursing Services.

"At the time, there were few hospitals with accredited continuing education programs for nurses, and I'm proud to have led our initiative and to have impacted education in that way," said Dille, a member of the American Nurses Association and the Indiana State Nurses Association since 1975.

That continuing education program, which received approval from the Indiana State Nurses Association and accreditation from the American Nurses Credentialing Center, is still offered by the IU Health system. Dille eventually shared her expertise with the ANCC where she served as a site appraiser for more than a dozen years, evaluating other such programs seeking accreditation.

Dille retired in 2012 after a sixteen-year stint with Eli Lilly and Company where she was a clinical research administrator, product associate in the Global Product Safety division, and associate consultant in the Global Regulatory Quality division.

After her retirement, Dille returned to IUPUI in a volunteer role as a member of the IUPUI University Library Community Board and continues to support student success and lifelong learning through the Claudia A. Dille Student Initiative Fund and the Claudia A. Dille Nursing Scholarship. In 2018, she received the IUPUI Spirit of

Claudia Dille. *Photo by Liz Kaye / Indiana University.*

Philanthropy Award for her decades-long commitment to the university and its students. In addition, Dille is an active volunteer in the local community, working with United Way of Central Indiana, the city of Fishers, and Heartland Film, which awarded her the 2018 President's Award for her service.

Above Claudia Dille stands with Jawz at the 2016 Regatta. *Photo courtesy of Claudia Dille.*

Facing top Campus Ambassadors and students representing Regatta and Jagathon pose with mascots Jinx, Jazzy, and Jawz near the IUPUI Talent Showcase stage during the 50th Anniversary Fall Kickoff Celebration. *Photo by Liz Kaye / Indiana University.*

Facing bottom Mascots, cheerleaders, and student leaders encourage the crowd during the IUPUI fight song during the 50th Anniversary Fall Kickoff Celebration Jaguar Spirit Fest. *Photo by Liz Kaye / Indiana University.*

Fall Kickoff Celebration
Jaguar Spirit Fest

IUPUI

1969–2019

Explosive Growth and Change

GLENN IRWIN RETIRED AS CHANCELLOR IN 1986. His successor was Gerald L. Bepko, dean of the IU School of Law–Indianapolis, followed in 2003 by Charles R. Bantz. Chancellors Bepko and Bantz oversaw a period of dramatic growth for the university, including IUPUI's move to NCAA Division I athletics competition, construction of the IUPUI Campus Center, record-breaking fund-raising campaigns, a 25 percent increase in enrollment, and a 100 percent increase in the number of full-time faculty.

With such transformation came a renewed need for coordinated and campuswide strategic planning to ensure that IUPUI faculty and staff worked in concert to achieve agreed-upon goals. In 2014, after an intensely collaborative process led by then-Executive Vice Chancellor Nasser H. Paydar, IUPUI launched its strategic plan, Our Commitment to Indiana and Beyond, which identified three key priorities: student success; advances in the health and life sciences; and contributions to the well-being of the citizens of Indiana, the state of Indiana, and beyond.

Facing IUPUI mascot Jazzy helps students, faculty, and staff kick off IUPUI's yearlong 50th Anniversary celebration on August 24, 2018. *Photo by Liz Kaye / Indiana University.*

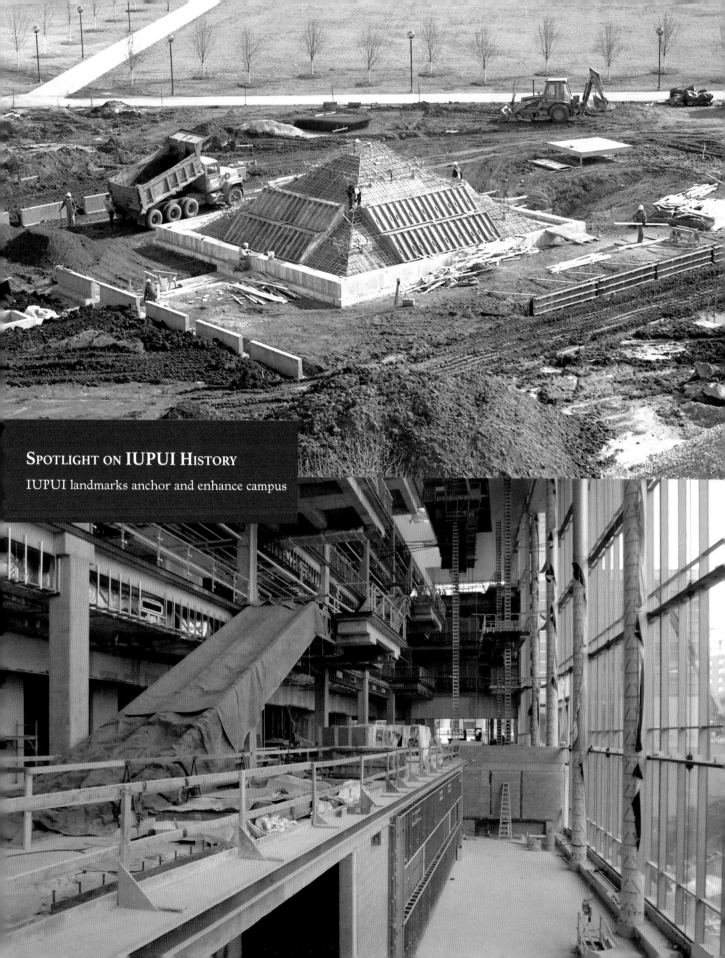

Gerald L. Bepko

Third Chancellor of IUPUI (1986–2002);
Dean Emeritus of the IU School of Law–Indianapolis

DURING THE SIXTEEN YEARS THAT Gerald "Jerry" Bepko served as chancellor of IUPUI, the campus experienced unprecedented growth, both in the dramatic expansion of the university's physical campus and in terms of the breadth of academic programs and research opportunities. While IUPUI was expanding under Bepko's leadership—from 1986 to 2002—major projects and improvements were transforming the city of Indianapolis.

Above Chancellor Bepko appears on a CBS Sports broadcast during the 1987 Pan American Games hosted by Indianapolis and IUPUI. *Photo courtesy of IUPUI Special Collections and Archives (UA24–002351n).*

Facing top Construction of Wood Fountain in 1995. *Photo courtesy of IUPUI Special Collections and Archives (295–6010–002).*

Facing bottom Construction of the Campus Center in 2008. *Photo courtesy of IU Studios.*

According to Chancellor Bepko, "Along with the city, IUPUI changed its mission and its aspirations."

Chancellor Bepko's vision ultimately established IUPUI as a leading urban university, ranked among the highest in its peer group, and an integral component of Central Indiana's research corridor. Bepko brought the various programs of IUPUI academically and geographically together on the downtown campus, and he oversaw the construction of almost two dozen buildings, including University Library, Inlow Hall, and the Engineering Science and Technology Building. His emphasis on undergraduate education culminated in the creation of University College in 1998.

During Bepko's tenure, enrollment grew by nearly 25 percent, and external support for faculty activities skyrocketed from $38 million in 1986 to more than $200 million in 2002. He led the first six years of the seven-year Campaign for IUPUI, which generated

From left: Richard D. and Billie Lou Wood, former IU President Myles Brand, and IUPUI Chancellor Bepko at the dedication of Wood Fountain in 1995. *Photo courtesy of IUPUI Special Collections and Archives (695–151–3).*

more than $1 billion before its conclusion in 2004, the first fund-raising campaign in Indiana to surpass the billion-dollar mark.

Following Bepko's service as chancellor, he was selected unanimously by the IU Board of Trustees to serve as interim president of Indiana University from January 1, 2003, to August 31, 2003. Bepko served in this role after the resignation of Myles Brand, who became president of the NCAA, and prior to the appointment of Adam Herbert as the seventeenth president of the university.

The campus community still feels Chancellor Bepko's positive impact. The IUPUI Bepko Scholars and Fellows Program provides a four-year scholarship for students who demonstrate integrity, leadership, and a commitment to service, and the Bepko Learning Center encourages students to play a key role in the academic development of their peers by applying collaborative learning techniques and facilitating group experiences.

Numerous university awards are named in his honor, including the IUPUI Bepko Staff Council Spirit Award, the Jean C. and Gerald L. Bepko Lifelong Learner Award, the Gerald L. Bepko Outstanding Administrator Award, and the Gerald L. Bepko IUPUI Community Medallion Award.

Bepko joined the IUPUI law faculty in 1972 and became a full professor in 1975. In 1979, he was named associate dean for academic affairs and became dean of the IU School of Law–Indianapolis—now known as the Robert H. McKinney School of Law—in 1981.

Among his many accolades, Bepko has received honorary degrees from IU, Purdue University, and the Illinois Institute of Technology Chicago–Kent College of Law. In 2015, he received the University Medal from IU President Michael A. McRobbie, the highest award bestowed by the university, for his extraordinary contributions and exceptional achievements.

Charles R. Bantz

Fourth Chancellor of IUPUI (2003–2015); Executive Vice President Emeritus of Indiana University; Professor of Communication Studies; Affiliate Faculty Member of the Lilly Family School of Philanthropy

CHARLES R. BANTZ LED THE IUPUI CAMPUS through a period of incredible growth for more than a decade, from 2003 until 2015. With an impressive increase in the campus's physical footprint as well as major changes to the student body, a notable expansion of research and creative activities, and a renewed commitment to diversity and inclusion, Bantz helped reinforce the role of IUPUI as a twenty-first-century university.

IUPUI's physical transformation during Bantz's tenure came in the form of expanded student housing, which allowed the number of students living on campus to grow from about 350 in 2003 to more than 2,400 today. The university also added research space with the construction of the Science and Engineering Laboratory Building in 2013.

Of all the buildings constructed during Bantz's time as chancellor, the Campus Center may have made the most dramatic difference. Beginning with its opening in 2008, it has provided students a home on campus, given them a selection of several restaurants, and offered them a place to hang out between classes.

In addition, while Bantz was chancellor, the number of bachelor's degrees conferred at IUPUI jumped by 66 percent, and the campus created ten new doctoral programs, ten additional master's programs, and eleven more bachelor's degree programs. During that same period, research funding

IUPUI's fourth chancellor, Charles R. Bantz.
Photo by Liz Kaye / Indiana University.

Chancellor Bantz joins Executive Vice Chancellor Uday Sukhatme in celebrating professor of educational leadership and policy studies Nancy Chism in 2012 on the occasion of her retirement. *Photo courtesy of IUPUI Special Collections and Archives (UA24_009811).*

grew by more than $120 million, and the campus significantly strengthened ties to the city through community and service learning, earning IUPUI a place on the US President's Higher Education Community Service Honor Roll several years in a row.

In 2015, IUPUI established the Charles R. Bantz Chancellor's Community Fellowship in recognition of his leadership and contributions to the campus and the city of Indianapolis. This grant reflects Bantz's dedication to research that embraces community-focused goals, creates partnerships, and results in local impact. In this way and many others, Chancellor Bantz was—and continues to be—driven by a desire to support and enhance IUPUI's positive impact on the neighborhoods that surround the campus.

Lorraine Blackman
Associate Professor Emerita, School of Social Work

WHEN DR. LORRAINE BLACKMAN, associate professor emerita of social work, joined the School of Social Work at IUPUI in 1992, she did so as a member of the largest cohort of African-American faculty in the university's history.

For more than two decades following her arrival at IUPUI, Blackman focused her teaching and research on shaping clinical social work practice with an emphasis on family life education for African Americans. A dedicated community activist and public servant, Blackman has devoted her academic career to one thing: strengthening families.

After getting a master of science in social work at the University of Tennessee–Knoxville, performing twenty years of social work practice, and then earning a doctorate from Florida State University, Blackman came to teach in Indianapolis. IUPUI's urban campus proved to be an ideal location for applying social work principles to community challenges.

"IUPUI was the perfect setting for civically engaged teaching, research, and service, as well as translational research. Every day was focused on improving the quality of life in our local and global community," she said.

Blackman's creative and inspiring teaching methods translated theories and evidence-based practice into practical applications. In the classroom, she often looked to news headlines to spark dialogue with her students and encouraged them to take what they learned in the classroom and apply that knowledge in tangible, relevant ways.

"I love the fact that we have students coming from real-life situations and coming from real communities in Indianapolis. They enrich the classroom experience especially with real-life problems," said Blackman. "One of the things we found to be very successful was using problem-based learning so that students were studying issues that were relevant to their communities and developing research-based solutions to problems in Indianapolis."

Her breadth of work and expertise in the area of family life education led Blackman to create the African American Family Life Education Institute. Located in Indianapolis, AAFLE offers a curriculum that teaches and promotes healthy, functioning families and has trained hundreds of people across the United States to implement its curricula.

Blackman continues to support local organizations that promote family health and healthy communities. She led a campus collaboration with the Indiana Minorities AIDS Coalition, the Marion County Health Department, the Indiana University School of Medicine, the Richard M. Fairbanks School of Public Health, and other partners exploring issues around adolescents with HIV/AIDS.

Lorraine Blackman among IUPUI students in the Business/SPEA Building.
Photo by Liz Kaye / Indiana University.

Blackman serves on the IUPUI Senior Academy Board and is the recipient of a Spirit of Philanthropy Award and an Outstanding Faculty Award. She has consulted with the US Department of Health and Human Services as well as the Administration for Children and Family Services for eight years. The author of numerous print and electronic publications, Blackman has also presented her research countless times, including at the Congressional Black Caucus Legislative Conference.

Kim Merritt

Interim Managing Director, IUPUI Alumni Relations; IUPUI Class of 1995, School of Science

"HAVING BEEN ON CAMPUS since I was a student, IUPUI feels like home to me," said IUPUI Interim Managing Director of Alumni Relations Kim Merritt. "I vividly remember leaving a psychology class during my senior year and thinking that I would like to work at IUPUI, in any capacity, someday."

Above Kim Merritt chats with retired IUPUI Alumni Relations colleague Sharon Holland. *Photo by Liz Kaye / Indiana University.*

Left Merritt poses after her graduation from the School of Science in 1995. *Photo courtesy of Kim Merritt.*

That was almost twenty-four years ago. When Merritt first joined the IUPUI staff shortly after her graduation from the School of Science, it was as an administrative assistant in the IU Center on Philanthropy. In 1997, she took a position in the IUPUI Office of Alumni Relations, and she has been an integral part of its team ever since.

While Merritt's day-to-day responsibilities vary throughout the year, creating and maintaining meaningful relationships with current students and IUPUI alumni are at the heart of her position. In her previous role as director of alumni programs, Merritt coordinated alumni programming and events for the Herron School of Art and Design, the School of Engineering and Technology, and the School of Science, and she organized award-winning programs like Herron's Visual Communication Design Conference and the IUPUI Top 100 Outstanding Undergraduate Student Recognition Program, among her other responsibilities. In her new position overseeing IUPUI Alumni Relations, Merritt's experience as an IUPUI alumna informs the strategy and vision she brings as she works to establish the critical connections that keep alumni actively engaged with IUPUI.

Stefan Davis, retired executive director of IUPUI Alumni Relations and associate vice president of the Indiana University Alumni Association, said of Merritt, "She has been a builder during her years working in Alumni Relations. She is constantly looking for opportunities to build both stronger and—more important—lasting relationships within our community of alumni, students, staff, and faculty. Her lead role in managing the Top 100 Program has helped establish a campus tradition, adding another layer to the IUPUI community."

"I love the sense of community at IUPUI. I'm fortunate to have worked with a great group of dedicated staff members and have formed friendships as a result of working so closely with different alumni groups over the years," Merritt said. "It is a privilege to get to work with individuals who have so many options in terms of where they can give back to their community. I never take for granted how special it is that they choose to make IUPUI one of those places."

Etta Ward

Assistant Vice Chancellor for Research and Development; IUPUI Class of 1995 and 2008, School of Liberal Arts

IUPUI's ASSISTANT VICE CHANCELLOR for Research and Development Etta Ward doesn't call her college journey unique, but it is certainly a story of hard work and perseverance. A married mother of two as an Indianapolis high school senior, Ward was determined to shape a successful future for herself and her family.

"Starting out as a teen mom came with a stigma and a specific narrative, based on the statistics," Ward said. "But my husband and I, by the grace of God, were determined to turn that narrative on its head. Through prayer and hard work, I was able to complete my undergraduate degree in English and even made the dean's list a few times. IUPUI was an important part of my life during this time."

Etta Ward in University Library. *Photo by Liz Kaye / Indiana University.*

After graduating with her bachelor's degree in English in 1995, Ward accepted a position with the March of Dimes in Indianapolis. Her rise through the ranks in that organization took her first to Marietta, Georgia, and then to Atlanta where she coordinated a number of statewide services.

Ward returned to IUPUI in 2002 and a year later assumed a directorship position in the Office of the Vice Chancellor for Research. During her years as director, and later executive director, Ward managed many grant programs supporting faculty research and helped to spearhead the Enhanced Mentoring Program with Opportunities for Ways to Excel in Research (EMPOWER), advancing the research activities of women and minority faculty. She eventually pursued a master's degree in philanthropic studies, which she earned in 2008.

Ward also helped create and launch IUPUI's first formal mentoring program for staff and is actively involved with national mentoring initiatives. In the fall of 2018, she gained a global perspective on effective mentorship in France as a Fulbright Scholar with the Council for International Exchange of Scholars.

"I smile when I think about how it has all come full circle. I now work with and support some of the same faculty who taught and encouraged me as an undergraduate and graduate student. I count many of them as mentors who guided me through pivotal junctures in my academic and professional journey here at IUPUI," Ward said.

Ward has been the recipient of several awards, including the IUPUI Multicultural Staff Impact Award, the Gerald L. Bepko Staff Council Spirit Award, and the United Way Diversity Advocate Award. As president of the School of Liberal Arts Alumni Association Board, she was also among the inaugural recipients of the IU Alumni Association Volunteer Leadership Award in 2019.

Ward chatting with colleague and friend Stephan Viehweg.
Photo by Liz Kaye / Indiana University.

James Kendrick
Stacks Manager, University Library;
IUPUI Class of 2004, School of Science

JAMES KENDRICK HAS BEEN A FIXTURE in IUPUI's University Library for more than thirty years, much longer than the library has been housed in the now-iconic building in the middle of the IUPUI campus. As stacks manager, Kendrick has touched thousands of books in the library's vast collection, which totals more than one million volumes. Over three decades, he has kept the collection orderly and accessible to generations of IUPUI students, faculty, and staff.

"James is a familiar face to many in the IUPUI community because he is outgoing, friendly, and always makes time to speak to everyone he sees," said John Cooper, circulation and security team supervisor at University Library.

James Kendrick. *Photo by Liz Kaye / Indiana University.*

Kendrick stands outside of University Library in front of Sasson Soffer's *East Gate/West Gate*, a public sculpture on loan from the Indianapolis Museum of Art. Of special note: the sculpture was transported from the IMA to its current location via helicopter in 2009. *Photo by Liz Kaye / Indiana University.*

Kendrick was born and raised in Indianapolis, and he has seen waves of change not just at IUPUI but also around the city. The youngest of nine children, he attended a segregated elementary school on Indianapolis's east side before graduating from Arsenal Technical High School. A work-study program in medical science first brought him to IUPUI in 1982. When he began his full-time career in the library in 1985, the campus consisted of far fewer buildings, and the library was housed in Taylor Hall.

In addition to being a staff member, Kendrick is now an alumnus and, again, a student. In 2004, he graduated from the School of Science with a bachelor's degree in psychology. He earned a graduate certificate in nonprofit management in 2016 and is pursuing a master of public administration degree, both from the Paul H. O'Neill School of Public and Environmental Affairs at IUPUI. He expects to receive his master's degree in time to celebrate his thirty-fifth anniversary with the university, every year in the same department at University Library.

Along with his integral role in the library as stacks manager, Kendrick is the library's United Way ambassador as well as a unit ambassador for the IUPUI Campus Campaign, a fund-raising campaign focused on faculty and staff. He is also a volunteer for Team IUPUI, which helps ensure new and continuing students have a smooth enrollment experience at the start of each semester.

"James reflects a love of service and of learning that he has expressed as a dedicated staff member, a lifelong learner, and an ambassador to University Library for IUPUI's United Way campaign," said Christine Fitzpatrick, former campaign cochair and retired chief of staff in the Office of the Chancellor. "I am inspired by his commitment to making the most of his experiences at IUPUI."

SPOTLIGHT ON THE 50TH ANNIVERSARY

Previous pages Aerial view of the IUPUI campus from White River with the Indianapolis skyline rising in the background. *Photo by James Brosher / Indiana University.*

Below The IUPUI Campus Center celebrated its tenth anniversary in 2018 and provides a vital gathering space for students, faculty, and staff on. *Photo by James Brosher / Indiana University.*

Above More than seventeen thousand people celebrated at the Campus Center on January 24, 2019, for IUPUI's official fiftieth birthday. *Photo by Liz Kaye / Indiana University.*

Following page Aerial view of IUPUI's iconic Wood Fountain.
Photo by James Brosher / Indiana University.

Spotlight on IUPUI History

University Hall rises at the corner of
New York Street and University Boulevard

2. CELEBRATING OUR PRESENT
Shaping the Campus of Today

THE IUPUI CAMPUS OF TODAY CELEBRATES and builds on the history of discovery, resourcefulness, growth, and change that distinguishes IUPUI as one of the premier urban research universities in the country. The key strategic priority that drives the campus forward is student success. This priority has resulted in IUPUI's national recognition for first-year programs and themed learning communities. It has led to IUPUI's honors as a top-twenty most innovative campus and home of outstanding undergraduate teaching from *U. S. News and World Report.*

Such recognition reflects IUPUI's ingenious and creative faculty and staff, who tailor their methods and resources to meet the needs of today's student. It also shines a spotlight on the achievements of IUPUI students who support and improve the campus community. From blazing new trails in digital scholarship to developing state-of-the-art 3-D printing to supporting research and education with cutting-edge data infrastructure, IUPUI looks around the corner to see what students—and the world—will need five, ten, or twenty years from now, always innovating with the future in mind.

Facing top. Construction on University Hall began in 2014. The building provides classroom space and is home to the Lilly Family School of Philanthropy, the School of Social Work, IUPUI Alumni Relations, the IU Foundation, and administrative offices. *Photo by Liz Kaye / Indiana University.*

Facing bottom University Hall is a LEED Gold-rated building that piloted IUPUI's desk-side recycling program and reinforces the campus's commitment to sustainability. *Photo by Liz Kaye / Indiana University.*

Left Faculty and staff who work in University Hall gather for a picture in the days prior to the building's 2015 dedication. *Photo by Liz Kaye / Indiana University.*

Nasser H. Paydar

Fifth Chancellor of IUPUI; Executive Vice President of Indiana University; Professor of Mechanical Engineering, School of Engineering and Technology

WHEN IUPUI'S FIFTH CHANCELLOR, NASSER H. PAYDAR, was just a teenager, his father impressed upon him the need to take his education as far as he could. That education would serve as Paydar's pathway to his future.

Paydar followed his father's advice, which took him thousands of miles from home to the State University of New York at Buffalo in 1975. He followed his soon-to-be wife, Niloo, when he transferred to Syracuse University soon thereafter. Ultimately, he received his bachelor's, master's, and doctoral degrees from the Department of Mechanical and Aerospace Engineering at Syracuse.

But Paydar's IUPUI story started even before he received his PhD from Syracuse. "In April of 1985, I received an offer from IUPUI to start as an assistant professor in the Department of Mechanical Engineering in Indianapolis," he explained. "I finished my studies in May, took a month off preparing for my first job here, and arrived in Indianapolis in July 1985 to start my career at IUPUI."

That career has endured for more than thirty years. As a faculty member, he served as principal and coprincipal investigator on research grants from federal and state agencies and private companies, including Cummins Electronics, the National Institutes of Health, the US Army, and the US Naval Air Warfare Center. His research in the area of solid mechanics, with applications in biomechanics and electronic packaging, has been widely published in scientific journals.

In addition, Paydar has held various administrative and executive leadership positions at Indiana University, including serving as vice chancellor and dean of IUPUC and chancellor of IU East where he oversaw dramatic gains in enrollment, first-year retention, and graduation rates.

In his position as executive vice chancellor and chief academic officer of IUPUI, to which he was appointed in 2012, Paydar led the university in a comprehensive and inclusive strategic planning process that resulted in the development of IUPUI's current strategic plan, Our Commitment to Indiana and Beyond.

As the fifth chancellor of IUPUI, Paydar has overseen dramatic changes on campus. Since 2015, IUPUI has formed two new schools: the School of Health & Human

Facing Nasser H. Paydar, fifth chancellor of IUPUI. *Photo by Liz Kaye / Indiana University.*

Chancellor Paydar busts a move with students at the IUPUI 50th Anniversary Birthday Bash on January 24, 2019. *Photo by Liz Kaye / Indiana University.*

Sciences and the School of Education. IUPUI has dedicated University Hall and North Residence Hall; has constructed two gateways to mark the eastern edge of campus; and has broken ground on Innovation Hall, a STEM education and research facility. It has completed a multimillion-dollar renovation of the Natatorium, considered by some to be the fastest swimming pool in the world, and partnered with the Madam Walker board with support from the Lilly Endowment on a major renovation of the Madam Walker Legacy Center on Indiana Avenue. The campus also celebrated its fiftieth anniversary from July 1, 2018, to June 30, 2019.

"Over the last fifty years, IUPUI has grown into the most comprehensive university campus in the state, offering Indiana University as well as Purdue degrees," Paydar said. "We have graduated more than 210,000 proud Jaguars, most of whom are from Indiana and stay in Indiana to live, learn, work, play, and contribute. For the 50th Anniversary year, we have taken advantage of the opportunity to tell our countless stories of success, and we look forward to the next fifty years."

Virginia Caine, MD

IU Bicentennial Professor; Associate Professor of Medicine, Department of Infectious Diseases; Adjunct Associate Professor, Fairbanks School of Public Health; Director, Marion County Public Health Department; Member, IUPUI Board of Advisors

ON APRIL 9, 2019, DR. VIRGINIA A. CAINE received IUPUI's 2019 Gerald L. Bepko Community Medallion in honor of her more than thirty years of exemplary application of research to critical public health problems. Over the years, Caine has built a national reputation for creating innovative programs to promote and advance positive public health outcomes.

Dr. Virginia Caine (left of center) with city and state leaders and local medical professionals who helped support the announcement of the Safe Syringe Initiative in Marion County. *Photo courtesy of Ruby Grosdidier.*

Dr. Virginia Caine. *Photo courtesy of Ruby Grosdidier.*

An infectious disease expert, Caine currently serves as director of the Marion County Public Health Department and in that role has been instrumental in addressing critical public health issues in Indianapolis and around the country. In 2018, she launched the Safe Syringe Access and Support Program to help reduce the transmission of hepatitis C and HIV, and in 2019, the health department joined community leaders and partners to unveil the mobile unit used to help operate the program.

Caine also created the first nationwide AIDS physician education program for the National Medical Association, a program later duplicated by the American Medical Association. Locally, she established the first HIV dental clinic in Marion County and the first countywide HIV/AIDS integrated health care delivery system involving major hospitals, community health centers, and social service agencies. As codirector of the Indianapolis Healthy Babies Initiative, she worked with community leaders to reduce the African-American infant mortality rate to its lowest level in the history of the city.

In 1984, Caine joined the staff at the IU School of Medicine as an assistant professor. Recognizing her accomplishments as well as her connection to and advocacy for the university, in 2018, she was named an IU Bicentennial Professor. Her pioneering and collaborative research has improved public health delivery system efficiencies and reduced health disparities. Her focus on infectious diseases (especially HIV/AIDS) the infant mortality rate, and childhood obesity has made a tangible, lasting, and life-altering impact.

In addition to her service on the IUPUI Board of Advisors, Caine has served on committees for the Centers for Disease Control and Prevention and the US Department of Health and Human Services. In 2004, she served as president of the American Public Health Association, the nation's oldest and largest public health organization, and she has also served in various capacities on the board of trustees for the National Medical Association, the Managed Emergency Surge for Healthcare Coalition, the IU Simon Cancer Center Community Advisory Committee, and the National Biodefense Science Board, among other appointments.

Caine has received numerous local, state, and national honors, including two Sagamore of the Wabash awards and the BioCrossroads Watanabe Life Sciences Champion of the Year award in 2017, among her many other accolades.

Kristi Palmer

Founding Herbert Simon Family Dean of University Library; IUPUI Class of 2003, School of Library and Information Science

Founding Herbert Simon Family Dean of University Library Kristi Palmer is all about connecting people to information, whether it is scholars to research, students to texts, or visitors to library resources. "My favorite thing about IUPUI is our community connectedness. We've really embraced that at University Library, and it's why I have stayed at IUPUI as long as I have," she said.

Palmer first became connected to IUPUI as a graduate student of library science, then assistant and associate librarian, followed by associate dean for digital scholarship, interim dean, and now dean of University Library. For seventeen years—fifteen of which she has served on the IUPUI faculty—Palmer has been a dedicated member

Dean Kristi Palmer performs a balancing act in the shelves of University Library at IUPUI.
Photo by Liz Kaye / Indiana University.

of the campus community, and since her days in graduate school, she has become a trusted expert on the library's team, especially in the area of digital scholarship.

"IUPUI has been a welcome constant in my educational and professional life for seventeen years," Palmer said. "I'm privileged to be part of a University Library staff that is committed and driven to fulfill our mission to inform, connect, and transform the IUPUI and Indianapolis community."

Palmer certainly shares in that commitment. As associate dean of digital scholarship, she led the development and implementation of the library's digital scholarship strategy, which supports the creation, digitization, and preservation of scholarly, historical, and cultural content. As director of the Center for Digital Scholarship, Palmer worked with colleague Jennifer Johnson to secure grant funding to support trailblazing 3-D-scanned collections with the Indianapolis Motor

Palmer shares a moment in the dean's office with Associate Dean for Collections at University Library Tina Baich. *Photo by Liz Kaye / Indiana University.*

Speedway Museum and the Benjamin Harrison Presidential Site. As interim dean, Palmer provided important experience and leadership during a period of transition for University Library, guiding its strategic direction, mission, and operations.

Palmer was honored with the *Indianapolis Business Journal*'s Forty Under 40 award in 2016. That same year, she collaborated with fellow IUPUI librarians Ted Polley and Caitlin Pollack in a National Endowment for the Humanities contest called the Chronicling America Data Challenge. The University Library project, "Chronicling Hoosier," which focused on tracing the origins of the word, won third place in the nationwide competition. In 2009, Palmer was named a *Library Journal* Mover and Shaker. In addition, she was the lead innovator on the IUPUI Welcoming Campus project "Windows to IUPUI's Past, Present, and Future," which visually depicts how our campus has evolved over the past fifty years.

David Nguyen
Assistant Professor, School of Education; IUPUI Class of 2006, McKinney School of Law and Kelley School of Business

DAVID NGUYEN CONTINUED HIS FAMILY'S IUPUI tradition and created a legacy. Born to Vietnamese immigrant parents just months after they settled in Indianapolis, Nguyen followed in his mother's footsteps when he chose IUPUI where he completed a joint JD/MBA degree at the Robert H. McKinney School of Law and the Kelley School of Business.

"IUPUI has a special place in my life. While learning a second language and acculturating to a new community, my mother graduated from IUPUI and the School of Science only years after resettling in Indianapolis. Her experience helped instill the importance of higher education in my family and demonstrated the difference that higher education can make for refugees in a new community. As much as IUPUI has given to me and my family, I try to give back equally by helping to support the university community through volunteer work as an alumnus."

Nguyen embodies the spirit of giving back. He served as the pro bono director of the American Bar Association's Disaster Legal Services Program, a position he held for several years. He is a past president of the IUPUI Alumni Advisory Council as well as an active alumni volunteer for the IUPUI Regatta. Through his contributions to his profession and IUPUI and his service to his communities, he continues to make a significant positive impact.

"I have seen this positive spirit in David since he was a law student," said Andrew Klein, former dean of the McKinney School of Law. "David always seeks to make his own community a better place, and I am proud to count him as one of our own."

After completing his JD/MBA, Nguyen was named visiting professor of business ethics at Vietnam National University in Ho Chi Minh City where he developed curriculum and taught graduate courses. As a recipient of the Rotary Foundation Ambassadorial Scholarship, he earned his master of advanced legal studies from Leiden University in the Netherlands followed by his doctorate in education policy studies from Indiana University. Most recently, he served as an assistant professor at

Facing David Nguyen with his mother after she graduated from the School of Science at IUPUI. *Photo courtesy of David Nguyen.*

Nguyen with his two sons, Santiago and Leo, and wife, Dr. Zelideh Martinez Hoy.
Photo courtesy of David Nguyen.

the University of Texas at San Antonio before returning to IUPUI in August 2018 as an assistant professor of urban education leadership and policy studies at the School of Education.

"Teaching higher education law and higher education management really meshes all three areas I've studied: law, business, and education," he said. "It's like I've come full circle." He and his wife, Dr. Zelideh Martinez Hoy, have two sons, Santiago and Leo.

Keith Anliker

Senior Lecturer, School of Science

IF YOU DON'T ALREADY FOLLOW KEITH ANLIKER on Twitter, you should. There, he celebrates his #FabStudents, dons his IUPUI 50th Anniversary baseball cap, and takes followers along on his adventures across campus and across the country. This is all in a day's work for Anliker, director of laboratory and curriculum support and senior lecturer in the Department of Chemistry and Chemical Biology at the School of Science.

Keith Anliker works in his office surrounded by IUPUI memorabilia collected over the course of his teaching career. *Photo by Liz Kaye / Indiana University.*

Anliker brings chemistry to life for his students using balloons.
Photo by Liz Kaye / Indiana University.

He began as a staff member more than thirty years ago and became faculty in 2002. Over the years, he has seen dramatic transformations in the city, on our campus, and in his classroom.

"In my time here, I've seen huge changes in IUPUI's infrastructure, but also in our students, faculty, and staff," Anliker said.

His adaptability to the ever-changing landscape of higher education and his ability to build and maintain meaningful relationships with students and faculty alike have contributed to his decades-long success at IUPUI.

"I just love higher education and how we do it at IUPUI. It is such an optimistic endeavor: new students all the time, new plans for our courses, new technologies, and new teaching methods that we are hopeful will improve student success," he said.

Anliker's teaching philosophy and approach to curriculum are focused on establishing relatable connections to chemistry and providing opportunities for student engagement that will contribute to their overall success. Anliker extends his impact through his role as coordinator of the Chemistry Resource Center, as faculty advisor for the IUPUI Chemistry Club, and as course coordinator for the Gateway to Graduation Program, a faculty-led effort to improve learning outcomes and retention for first-year students.

Anliker has been honored time and again for his excellence in teaching with awards including the Chancellor's Award for Excellence in Teaching, the School of Science Lecturer Service Award, the University College Trustees Teaching Award, and the Glenn W. Irwin Jr., MD, Experience Excellence Award. He was inducted into the Faculty Academy on Excellence in Teaching in 2007 and serves on its steering committee to help promote and sustain teaching and learning excellence at IUPUI.

Simon J. Rhodes, former dean of the School of Science, said, "Keith is one of those special people who bring dedication and commitment to all aspects of our mission. He is an outstanding teacher who is devoted to student success, he is a valued faculty member in the School of Science who always works for the general good, and his enthusiasm in the academic domain makes me very proud to be his colleague."

"I have truly been able to live my dream at IUPUI because of the wonderful people who have supported me and because of the students I've gotten to know and connect with," Anliker said. "I hope that IUPUI can continue to be a place where students grow and excel for the next fifty years."

Khalilah Shabazz
Assistant Vice Chancellor for Student Diversity, Equity and Inclusion; Director, IUPUI Multicultural Center; Founding Director, Diversity Enrichment and Achievement Program; IUPUI Class of 2000, School of Science

Dr. Khalilah Shabazz, assistant vice chancellor for student diversity, equity, and inclusion, likens her transformative journey from an eighteen-year-old single parent to a doctor of higher education to that of a butterfly. Born and raised in Indianapolis, Shabazz was determined to shatter the stereotype of an uneducated and unproductive Black teenage mother. In 2000, she became the first in her family to graduate from college when she earned a bachelor of science in psychology from the School of Science at IUPUI.

Her passion for education and her desire to work with students like herself propelled her to a master of science and doctorate in higher education and student affairs from the School of Education at IU Bloomington.

During her seventeen-year career at IUPUI, Shabazz has focused much of her work on supporting and retaining minority student populations. She joined the IUPUI staff as the scholarship coordinator in the Office of Student Scholarships and soon thereafter was promoted to assistant director for student retention and scholarship. As founding director of the Diversity Enrichment and Achievement Program, Shabazz developed and implemented concepts and strategies to promote the success of under-represented students at IUPUI.

In 2014, Shabazz became the second director of the IUPUI Multicultural Center, and she retains that directorship in her new role as assistant vice chancellor. As AVC, Shabazz draws on her extensive experience and training, overseeing student diversity and inclusion efforts with the goal of ensuring that IUPUI fosters a climate where all students feel like they belong and can succeed, especially students from underrepresented backgrounds. Shabazz's continuing role at the Multicultural Center keeps her well connected to the people and programming that—together—will help her strengthen diverse student support and retention efforts as she works with partners across campus to diversify the curriculum.

"Our students have stories and journeys that they share with us, and it is an absolute pleasure to be part of their academic, personal, and social development while they're

Shabazz chats with colleagues from the Multicultural Center. *Photo by Liz Kaye / Indiana* University.

here on campus," she said. "I hope that IUPUI will continue to celebrate the rich cultural history of our institution and the diversity of our campus for future generations."

In addition to her work at the Multicultural Center, Shabazz teaches courses on diversity and multiculturalism for the School of Education and University College and codirects the Sankofa: A Cultural Journey through Ghana study abroad program. She also conducts cultural competency workshops in the community and is the founder of Student African American Sisterhood National Organization Inc., an eighteen-chapter national nonprofit dedicated to the development of young women of color in the educational pipeline.

Khalilah Shabazz holds a picture of herself from when she was a freshman at IUPUI in the 1990s. *Photo courtesy of Khalilah Shabazz.*

Shabazz's accomplishments have been widely recognized. She is the recipient of the Susan Buck Sutton Study Abroad Award, the Black Student Union Advocate of the Dream Award, the Alvin S. Bynum Award for Excellence in Academic Mentoring, the IU Neal-Marshall Distinguished Alumni Award, and the Glenn W. Irwin Jr., MD, Experience Excellence Award.

Shannon McCullough
Assistant Dean of Admissions and Student Affairs, Herron School of Art and Design; IUPUI Class of 2004, School of Science, and Class of 2016, School of Education

WHEN SHANNON MCCULLOUGH GRADUATED with her doctoral degree in higher education and student affairs in 2016, she made history as one of eight women of color to receive a PhD from the School of Education at IUPUI that year. "The Great Eight," as this cohort came to be known, is the largest group of African-American women to receive doctorates from the same school at the same time on the IUPUI campus, affirming their accomplishment and cementing their legacy. To commemorate their graduation, the women created the Great Eight Scholarship to support other graduate students—especially Black women—pursuing degrees in the School of Education at IUPUI.

The Great Eight at IUPUI. Front row, from left: Nadrea Njoku, Jasmine Haywood, Johari Shuck, Shannon McCullough, Tiffany Kyser; Back row, from left: Jada Phelps Moultrie, Juhanna Rogers, and Demetrees Hutchins. *Photo courtesy of News at IU.*

For McCullough, receiving her doctoral degree was a remarkable and humbling distinction that was years in the making. As an undergraduate psychology student in the School of Science at IUPUI, she got involved with a new program at the Bepko Learning Center called Structured Learning Assistance. In 2001, she became one of the program's first psychology peer mentors. Through that experience, she discovered a love and talent for mentoring that propelled her academic and professional career.

"That program became the subject of my doctoral research, so that's a big point of pride for me," she said.

After receiving her undergraduate degree from the School of Science, McCullough returned to the Bepko Learning Center and brought her passion for mentoring, first as coordinator of science mentor initiatives, then as assistant director of academic support services, and finally as the center's associate director until 2013. Mentorship remained a core focus in each of these positions, which encompassed course instruction, curriculum development and assessment, student recruitment, and cross-departmental collaboration and planning.

Now serving as assistant dean of admissions and student affairs at the Herron School of Art and Design, McCullough provides strategic vision and leadership on enrollment management, student access and retention, and academic success at both the undergraduate and graduate levels. In addition, she oversees the student affairs programming, including cocurricular and engagement activities and, of course, the school's mentoring initiatives.

"I came to IUPUI in 1999 for my undergraduate degree. Since then, not only have I advanced through three degrees on this campus, I also began my path in a professional career in academia," McCullough said. "I am very proud to be at IUPUI. I'm a Jaguar through and through."

McCullough sits in a studio at the Herron School of Art and Design. *Photo by Liz Kaye / Indiana University.*

Jake Manaloor

IUPUI Class of 2000, Kelley School of Business, and Class of 2003, McKinney School of Law

An accomplished student by anyone's standards, IUPUI alumnus Jake Manaloor had a triple major at the Kelley School of Business in business management, human resources management, and international studies, along with a minor in economics. This two-time Top 100 Outstanding Student was also a two-term president of Undergraduate Student Government. And that was just during his undergraduate years. Manaloor went on to receive his juris doctorate degree from the IU School of Law–Indianapolis in 2003, the same year he received the Norman Lefstein Award of Excellence for the more than one thousand hours of pro bono service he had provided.

Jake Manaloor poses in costume as Jinx during IUPUI's homecoming celebration in 2000. *Photo courtesy of IUPUI Special Collections and Archives (UA24–006828n).*

Manaloor at Roman ruins in Amman, Jordan. *Photo courtesy of Jake Manaloor.*

In addition to his academic pursuits, Manaloor worked at the Student Center, located in Taylor Hall at the time, and at the Natatorium's information desk where he quickly became friends with many of the student-athletes who walked its halls to and from training and practice.

"Because IUPUI students were paying the same athletic fees as students attending NCAA Division I schools, we wanted students attending IUPUI to have the opportunity to compete in and support that same level of competition. USG made inquiries to university athletics, campus administration, and the IU trustees regarding why the university could not have more than one Division I school, similar to many other top-tier institutions. Leadership heard and acknowledged our message; IUPUI started its transition to Division I in 1997," said Manaloor.

Following the campus's shift to Division I athletic competition, Undergraduate Student Government, led by Manaloor, advocated for a recognizable new logo and mascot that would unify students and alumni and give the Indianapolis community something to rally around. The now-familiar roaring Jaguar was unveiled on November 13, 1998, at The Jungle, and the Jaguar mascot was born. By popular student vote, Jinx was named and made his first official appearance in 1999.

And who better to don the new Jinx costume than Manaloor, who had been an important part of bringing the vision to reality? As the first Jinx mascot, Manaloor spent time at campus and community events like Jam the Jaguar Bus, Reading with Jaguar Athletes at Riley Hospital for Children, Race for the Cure, the 500 Festival Mini Marathon, and more.

"Seeing the projects that our USG team worked on come to successful fruition has been so cool. To see things like the UITS twenty-four-hour computer lab, the completion of the Campus Center and the vibrancy it now has, the Jaguars playing basketball games at a large venue like Indiana Farmers Coliseum, the growth of student-led activities like Jagathon and Regatta. These are my favorite memories of IUPUI," Manaloor said.

Facing top IUPUI mascots remain a compelling and energizing presence at a wide variety of campus events, including Jazzy at the Weeks of Welcome Ice Cream Social. *Photo by Liz Kaye / Indiana University.*

Facing bottom Jazzy and Jawz light up the dance floor at the IUPUI Birthday Bash on January 24, 2019. *Photo by Liz Kaye / Indiana University.*

Creating a More Welcoming and Inclusive Campus

LAUNCHED IN THE SPRING OF 2016, the Welcoming Campus Initiative has provided a springboard for transforming IUPUI into a more inspiring destination for faculty, staff, students, and visitors. With task forces, focus groups, and town hall meetings, the campus has sought to answer the question "How can we make IUPUI a more welcoming campus?"

Tied to IUPUI's strategic goals, this initiative has touched the lives of thousands of people who have planned or participated in dozens of innovative projects, several of which are reflected in the pages that follow. Projects range from a celebration of dance to mentoring initiatives, from e-sports competitions to the Japanese Olympiad of Indiana. Each one was designed not only to improve campus but also to strengthen the collaborations that lead to unexpected innovations.

Of course, the spirit of a welcoming and inclusive campus extends well beyond this initiative at IUPUI, guiding the way Jaguars treat one another, care for the physical environment, and partner with organizations across the city to improve the neighborhoods we share.

Facing top Executive Associate Dean of the School of Informatics and Computing Mathew Palakal speaks at the groundbreaking for IUPUI's Innovation Hall, a multidisciplinary classroom building that provides space for the STEM disciplines in the School of Science, the School of Engineering and Technology, and the School of Informatics and Computing. The ceremony took place April 23, 2019. *Photo by Liz Kaye / Indiana University.*

Facing bottom The ceremonial turning of dirt at the groundbreaking of Innovation Hall with IU Trustee James T. Morris, IUPUI Chancellor Paydar, IU Trustee MaryEllen Bishop, and IU President Michael A. McRobbie. *Photo by Liz Kaye / Indiana University.*

SPOTLIGHT ON IUPUI HISTORY

Student life brings energy, ice cream, and friendship

Above Members of student dance troupe The Moving Company at IUPUI share the joy of dance with youngsters at the Indianapolis Civic Theatre. *Photo courtesy of IUPUI Special Collections and Archives (UA24–004755).*

Facing top The annual ice cream social has become a time-honored tradition at IUPUI, held each fall for more than forty years. *Photo courtesy of IUPUI Special Collections and Archives.*

Facing bottom IUPUI students relax in their room at Ball Residence Hall, some of them knitting, circa 1970. *Photo courtesy of IUPUI Special Collections and Archives (UA24–005122s).*

Damon Spight
Academic Support Specialist, School of Dentistry

DAMON SPIGHT, FACULTY RECRUITMENT MANAGER in the Office of Faculty Affairs at the IU School of Dentistry, is so inspired by IUPUI's mission and culture that he has returned to join the staff not once but twice. He began his career at IUPUI more than twenty-five years ago in what was then the Office of the Vice Chancellor for Undergraduate Education. He left for a year before returning as outreach coordinator in what was the Office of Learning Partnerships, a position he held for a short time before spending the next ten years with the National FFA Organization. When he returned to IUPUI a second time, in 2011, it was to assume his current position.

"What attracted me to IUPUI in the beginning and led to my eventual return is the culture of learning and growth, not only for students but also for staff and administration," said Spight. "The collaborative nature of campus, the availability of cutting-edge technology, and the professional development opportunities, particularly in the School of Dentistry, are exceptional."

In addition to his role addressing faculty concerns, responding to employee policy inquiries, overseeing candidate recruitment processes, and tending to search committee needs in the School of Dentistry, Spight has made important contributions across campus. He was a member of the inaugural cohort for the Next Generation 2.0 Leadership Program, which prepares women and underrepresented faculty and staff for leadership positions and opportunities for advancement in higher education. That experience led Spight toward subsequent opportunities at IUPUI, including his participation in the school's working group on change and innovation and his service on the 50th Anniversary Steering Committee.

Gail Williamson, professor emerita of dental diagnostic sciences, said, "Damon is dedicated, disciplined, and meticulous in his work and a consummate professional when dealing with faculty, staff, and students alike. His reputation is exemplary, so he is sought after to serve on various school and campus committees and to support various initiatives and special projects. Several years ago, he was selected by the School of Dentistry to participate in the Next Generation 2.0 Leadership Program, which has served him well as he continues to contribute his time and talents to the school and campus."

By his own account, Spight's most significant professional achievement is his involvement in the creation of the first IUPUI Staff Mentoring Program, an idea that was

Facing Damon Spight relaxes in the School of Dentistry at IUPUI. *Photo by Liz Kaye / Indiana University.*

Spight chats with his colleague Meredith Lecklider in the School of Dentistry at IUPUI.
Photo by Liz Kaye / Indiana University.

born during his Next Generation 2.0 experience. Spight, along with others including Williamson and Assistant Vice Chancellor for Research Development Etta Ward, also a Face of IUPUI, engaged and collaborated with key campus stakeholders to give structure to the idea to match an established IUPUI faculty or staff member with a newer employee for a yearlong mentorship. The program, which was partially funded by a Welcoming Campus Innovation Fund grant, was a tremendous success during its first year, promising continued growth in the future.

"Damon truly understands the value and power of an effective mentoring relationship to help position professionals for success," Ward said. "He was integral in spearheading the effort to get buy-in at the highest level for IUPUI's first campuswide staff mentoring program. From the time we first met as former members of the IUPUI Staff Council to the present, spreading the mentoring message has been a consistent theme for Damon."

Cindy Harkness

Strategic Outreach and Community Partnerships Coordinator, Division of Enrollment Management

THE DIVISION OF ENROLLMENT MANAGEMENT'S strategic outreach and community partnerships coordinator Cindy Harkness is a well-known face around the IUPUI campus, recognizable to students, faculty, and staff for her warm, outgoing personality and her ever-present smile. An enthusiastic and proud ambassador for the university and its students, as well as for the city of Indianapolis, Harkness exemplifies IUPUI's welcoming spirit.

A native of Lafayette, Indiana, she attended DePauw University before graduating from Purdue University with a degree in communications science. Harkness—also known around town as "Indy Cindy"—began her IUPUI career seventeen years ago as the part-time services coordinator at the IUPUI Glendale Center.

Cindy Harkness (second from right) with a group of former campus ambassadors at the 2016 IUPUI Night at the Indiana Pacers basketball game. *Photo by Liz Kaye / Indiana University.*

Harkness sits in her office at the IUPUI Campus Center. *Photo by Liz Kaye / Indiana University.*

"After the interview, I met a wonderful lady outside of the IUPUI Glendale Center. We chatted about children, dogs, and life in general. Little did I know then that my nice new friend was Amy Conrad Warner, who at that time was the director of the IUPUI Community Learning Network. I have truly gotten to know and work with some of the best people at IUPUI," Harkness said.

"Cindy radiates the characteristics of a welcoming campus, and she works tirelessly to create an environment where our students are successful and confident personally, academically, and professionally," said Warner, now the vice chancellor for community engagement.

In her current role as strategic outreach and community partnerships coordinator, Harkness works with partners across the Office of Undergraduate Admissions to bring prospective students to campus for a firsthand look at what it means to be a Jaguar. She also advocates for IUPUI in the Indianapolis community, extending the university's reach to potential students. One such student is Paul H. O'Neill School of Public and Environmental Affairs alumnus André Zhang Sonera, also a Face of IUPUI, who met Harkness at the 2010 National FFA Organization convention in downtown Indianapolis where she told him about the programs and opportunities that IUPUI could offer a small-town boy from Puerto Rico.

"Ms. Harkness shared with me this board game poster that laid out the path for a student to apply and graduate from IUPUI. I remember taking that poster and hanging it on my wall, fantasizing and imagining what my life would be like if I were a Jaguar," said Zhang Sonera, who earned his bachelor's degree from IUPUI and is working on his master's degree in the O'Neill School.

"Students here have the unique opportunity to share ideas, engage in programs on campus and in the community, and truly develop their dreams. The sky is the limit at IUPUI," Harkness said.

Wilhelmenia Warren
Custodian, Campus Facility Services

WILHELMENIA WARREN, A VALUED MEMBER of the Campus Facilities team that provides service to more than sixty IUPUI buildings and three hundred acres of space, helps to create an inviting and welcoming campus environment for students, faculty, staff, and visitors. This beautiful campus, with landscaped greenspaces, state-of-the-art buildings, and well-maintained facilities, is due in part to Warren's hard work and dedication.

Warren, who joined the Custodial Services staff in 2015, takes pride in the work she does to clean and maintain order on the fourth and fifth floors of University Hall. But for her, it is also about the people with whom she interacts during her shift.

"I am a people person who enjoys meeting and greeting people each day, and the people here are friendly and very open-hearted. I love encouraging others, and to see people smile brightens my day," she said.

Wilhelmenia Warren is an important part of maintaining IUPUI's beautiful campus. *Photo by Liz Kaye / Indiana University.*

Warren cleans on the fourth floor of University Hall during her shift.
Photo by Liz Kaye / Indiana University.

The feeling is mutual. Warren's infectious smile and friendly nature have a positive impact on everyone with whom she interacts.

"It's always a pleasure to see Wilhelmenia at the end of the day; she consistently greets me with a smile. Her hard work and attention to detail make our work environment much more pleasant and stress free. She is thorough and conscientious, and it's obvious that she takes pride in her work. She has really become a trusted member of our family," said Shirley Yorger, senior administrative secretary in the Office of Planning and Institutional Improvement.

Prior to joining IUPUI, Warren worked in building services at the *Indianapolis Star* for twenty-seven years. In the late 1980s, before starting her career at the *Star*, Warren worked on campus at what was then University Place Hotel and Conference Center. A native of Indianapolis, she grew up spending her free time on Indiana Avenue, or "the Avenue," as it was commonly referred to at the time, and visiting the businesses that lined the popular corridor.

Josh Skillman
Associate Dean of Students; Director of Housing and Residence Life

IN THE LAST FIFTY YEARS, IUPUI HAS EVOLVED into a vibrant urban university with thriving residential communities serving more than 2,400 students. As associate dean of students and director of IUPUI Housing and Residence Life, Josh Skillman knows his job is to make those students feel at home in their IUPUI housing and help them establish and build strong campus connections.

It is a responsibility that Skillman, a native of Owensboro, Kentucky, takes quite seriously. His own college experience was shaped by his Residence Life team at Indiana University Bloomington, which was instrumental in helping him adjust and thrive as an undergrad. When Skillman was ready to drop out of college altogether, it was his resident assistant who supported him and encouraged him to stay in school. Because of that tremendous personal impact, Skillman has devoted his professional career to

Josh Skillman outside of IUPUI's historic Ball Hall. *Photo by Liz Kaye / Indiana University.*

student affairs, university housing, and residence life.

Since his graduation from IU with a master's degree in higher education and student affairs, he has worked on a number of different campuses. Starting at the University of Georgia, Skillman then spent nine years on staff at IUPUI in the Office of Housing and Residence Life. He played a critical role in the opening of North Residence Hall in 2016, ushering in a new era of campus life at IUPUI. North Hall was the first traditional residence hall built on campus since IUPUI was established in 1969.

For a brief period, Skillman left IUPUI for the Georgia Institute of Technology, but he returned in 2018 as director of Housing and Residence Life.

"My favorite thing about IUPUI is the energy and the passion that the students have here, and how eager they are to work with faculty and staff and let us be a part of their IUPUI experience," he said.

Skillman loves working in Housing and Residence Life because of the opportunity to make a positive impact on students living on campus as well as on the staff members working toward that goal every day.

Skillman takes a break on a luggage trolley in University Tower. *Photo by James Brosher / Indiana University.*

"I hope that the spirit of working together and the passion, excitement, and pride for IUPUI continues to grow over the next fifty years like it has over the last fifty. Of course, being a housing person, I hope that our program continues to grow so we can accommodate all of the students who want to live on campus at IUPUI," he said.

IUPUI also holds a special place in Skillman's personal life. His wife, Sarah, works on the IUPUI campus, and their two kids have attended the IUPUI Center for Young Children.

Meghan Nowels

Welcoming Campus Innovator Project Lead, A Celebration of Dance; IUPUI Class of 2020, School of Health & Human Sciences; President, The Moving Company at IUPUI

TOURISM, CONVENTIONS, AND EVENT management major Meghan Nowels knew IUPUI was home the moment she stepped into the Campus Center.

"During the campus tour, I kept picturing myself on this campus, going to classes and living in the dorms. I could see it all so perfectly in my head. When I toured other campuses, I just couldn't picture myself there. Something always felt a little bit off," she said.

Meghan Nowels. *Photo by Liz Kaye / Indiana University.*

IUPUI just felt right for the native of Kendallville, Indiana, and the university's academic programs sealed the deal. For a student pursuing tourism, conventions, and event management along with a minor in philanthropic studies, IUPUI provides the ideal combination of academic opportunities set against Indianapolis's urban energy.

"It just made sense. Indianapolis hosts great conventions and events. I have had amazing opportunities to volunteer at some of these events, like the National FFA Organization convention. Indianapolis is also home to the Lilly Family School of Philanthropy, the first and best school of philanthropy in the country. IUPUI was the right choice for me, and I am so thankful I became a Jag," she said.

Her favorite thing about IUPUI, though, is the extensive and diverse selection of student organizations through which students can get involved.

"Getting involved in student orgs really helps bring your college experience full circle," she said.

She found her home at The Moving Company at IUPUI, through which she has made lifelong friends and continued her love of dancing. She has also gained valuable

The Moving Company shares a Jaguar roar before rehearsal. *Photo by Liz Kaye / Indiana University.*

personal and professional development skills through her role as president of the dance group.

Director of The Moving Company at IUPUI Paige Prill Craigie describes Nowels saying that "her passion for dance is evidenced in her work ethic and her commitment. When Meghan moves, you can see her heart. As an officer for The Moving Company, she is an organizational mastermind."

Nowels takes her leadership role seriously. "My mission as The Moving Company president this year is to spread the love of dance across campus," she said.

And she is well on her way to accomplishing that. On behalf of The Moving Company, Nowels authored a Welcoming Campus Innovation Fund grant for A Celebration of Dance, a collaborative project featuring all of IUPUI's dance organizations and honoring the art of dance through a series of on-campus workshops, demonstrations, and performances that took place in the spring of 2019.

Sohin Shah

Welcoming Campus Innovator Project Co-Lead, UPnGO: An Initiative to Create a More Welcoming Campus for Graduate and Professional Students; IUPUI Class of 2019, School of Engineering and Technology

As an international student from India, Sohin Shah moved halfway around the world to pursue his master of science degree in mechanical engineering at the School of Engineering and Technology at IUPUI. Shah was at times unsure about living on his own for the first time in a new city, away from familiar people and places, but the diverse community he discovered in Indianapolis and at IUPUI quickly embraced him and gave him a sense of belonging.

Sohin Shah and classmate Argun Ambasana work on a vehicle prototype.
Photo by Liz Kaye / Indiana University.

Shah became part of the Jaguar community through his work in the Graduate Office among many other activities. *Photo by Liz Kaye / Indiana University.*

"Sohin is an amazing testament to the spirit of IUPUI: a school where you can come in without knowing anyone and engage in the campus community to have an enriching university experience," said Tabitha Hardy, assistant dean for student development and academic affairs in the IUPUI Graduate Office.

Shah's academic accomplishments and engagement on campus—in just two short years—are remarkable. But he is proudest of the relationships he has fostered and the friendships he has built. His work as a graduate assistant in the IUPUI Graduate Office, as a graduate emissary for student diversity, and as interim president of the Underrepresented Professional and Graduate Student Organization (UPnGO) has been foundational to many of those relationships.

"Sohin is truly an asset to the IUPUI community," Hardy said. "He has been invaluable in planning events for IUPUI's graduate students, including a mixer during Weeks of Welcome, the Preparing Future Faculty and Professionals Pathways Conference, the

Getting You Through Graduate School Professional Development Series, and countless others."

Shah was also a 2018 Welcoming Campus Innovator, co-leading the project Get UPnGO: An Initiative to Create a More Welcoming and Inclusive Campus for Graduate and Professional Students with Hardy.

As a mechanical engineering student with a concentration in mechatronics, Shah is passionate about technology and robotics. Mechatronics focuses on electrical and mechanical engineering systems that create design solutions using robotics, electronics, and telecommunications, among other specialty areas. Those passions led to Shah's assistantship at the Mechatronics Research Lab and to his involvement with the IUPUI agBOT Challenge team, which participates in an annual series of competitions that encourage innovation in robotics and agriculture. The team's autonomous agricultural robot earned it a second-place finish in the 2018 competition.

With his graduate degree in hand, Shah hopes to take his knowledge and research experience into the field of robotics while likely staying close to Indianapolis.

"I truly believe that with the right application, many of the world's problems can be solved by collaborating with robots," he said. "During my career, I aim to find solutions to some of these problems in hopes of a brighter future for everyone. I also hope to be continually involved with academia and contribute to preparing the next generation of engineers and scientists."

Following page top Students line up for the IUPUI Ice Cream Social, a campus tradition dating back to 1977. *Photo by Liz Kaye / Indiana University.*

Following page bottom With an IUPUI #JagsRoar graphic in the background, students gather at Carroll Stadium for Weeks of Welcome Light Up the Night. *Photo by Liz Kaye / Indiana University.*

SPOTLIGHT ON THE 50TH ANNIVERSARY

IUPUI launches the fall semester

Connecting with the Community

Chancellor Nasser H. Paydar has often said that service and engagement are in IUPUI's DNA. Such connections have been strengthened by the hundreds of thousands of community-service hours IUPUI students have contributed through coursework, internships, and research projects. IUPUI faculty seek out community partners with whom they work to develop mutually beneficial projects that have the potential for far-reaching impact.

This great strength of the IUPUI campus has been recognized nationally as well. In 2006, IUPUI was one of seventy-six colleges and universities in the United States to be selected for the Carnegie Foundation for the Advancement of Teaching's new Community Engagement Classifications. IUPUI was also one of only three universities awarded the US President's Higher Education Community Service Honor Roll Award for Excellence in General Community Service, the highest federal recognition an institution can receive for its commitment to community, service learning, and civic engagement.

The following Faces of IUPUI reflect the deep mutual commitment that exists between IUPUI and its many local partners.

Previous page top IUPUI Regatta representatives Jordan Martinez, Khrisma McMurray, and Kole Loehmer staff the oars and table at the 2018 Weeks of Welcome Involvement Fair. *Photo by Liz Kaye / Indiana University.*

Previous page bottom Chancellor Paydar joins IUPUI Housing and Residence Life staff on move-in day at historic Ball Hall. More than 2,400 IUPUI students live on campus. *Photo by Liz Kaye / Indiana University.*

Facing top An IUPUI basketball player reads with students at a local elementary school. *Photo courtesy of IUPUI Special Collections and Archives (UA24–007472).*

Facing bottom IUPUI representatives gather with community members for the 1995 opening of the Maternity Outreach and Mobilization Office in the Haughville neighborhood, just west of the IUPUI campus. *Photo courtesy of IUPUI Special Collections and Archives (995-6277-009).*

Following pages IUPUI faculty, staff, and students gather for the 2001 Martin Luther King Jr. Day of Service at the *Landmark for Peace* memorial sculpture in Dr. Martin Luther King Jr. Park north of downtown Indianapolis. *Photo courtesy of IUPUI Special Collections and Archives.*

Rafael Sanchez
RTV6 Investigative Reporter

RTV6's EMMY AWARD–WINNING consumer investigative reporter and news anchor Rafael Sanchez is an unapologetic, no-nonsense consumer advocate. Getting justice for those who have been taken advantage of is one of his passions. Another passion is giving back to the Indianapolis community that he has adopted as his own. In this, Sanchez shares a great deal with IUPUI where he has appeared on numerous occasions to support the university as well as causes that help transform neighborhoods and improve lives.

When he is in front of the camera, Sanchez is relentless and unflinching in his journalistic pursuit to right wrongs and find the truth. But his sometimes-intimidating television persona is just one facet of this multidimensional man. He is also a baseball dad, a ballroom dancer, and a fun-loving jokester who doesn't take himself too seriously, especially in the name of community service.

As co-emcee of the 2018 Indiana Black Expo Corporate Luncheon, sponsored by Indiana University, Sanchez donned a pineapple-printed suit and rode a bicycle around the Indiana Convention Center. His goal? To encourage people to fill the donation envelopes on every table with contributions to the many community programs and initiatives that IBE supports.

In his role as community engagement cochair for United Way of Central Indiana, an organization to which the university has a deep and lasting commitment, Sanchez emceed the IUPUI United Way Campaign Kickoff Luncheon in 2016, sporting light-up shoes and an Uncle Sam hat, and again in 2017, wearing a jacket patterned with $100 bills. In many different ways, Sanchez lights up any room he enters and draws attention to the ways people can give back to the community. The takeaway from his charitable work, he says, is that "everyone has time and talents to contribute to the community. You don't have to be rich or famous or even a good dancer."

"Rafael personifies the community focus of both the IUPUI and United Way missions. He brings laughter and fun to our United Way Campaign Kickoff Luncheon while helping us see the possibilities to make a real difference in a celebratory yet encouraging way," said Stephan Viehweg, cochair of IUPUI's United Way campaign, assistant research professor in the Department of Pediatrics at the IU School of Medicine, and associate director of the IUPUI Center for Translating Research Into Practice.

Facing Rafael Sanchez. *Photo courtesy of Rafael Sanchez.*

Sanchez at the 2017 IUPUI United Way Kickoff Luncheon. *Photo by Liz Kaye / Indiana University.*

Originally from the Bronx, Sanchez has been a fixture in Indianapolis for more than twenty years. He participates in dozens of charitable events around Central Indiana each year for causes that increase financial stability, decrease food insecurity and homelessness, and improve educational opportunities, among others.

He is the recipient of many awards for excellence in journalism, including Best Metro TV Reporter awards from the Associated Press and Best Consumer Reporting awards from the Society of Professional Journalists. Sanchez has also been recognized for his civic involvement by the Center for Leadership Development, Forest Manor Multicultural Center, Ronald McDonald House, and the Mozel Sanders Foundation.

Merlin Gonzales
Founder and President, Faith Hope and Love Community Inc.

MERLIN GONZALES BELIEVES IN THE POWER of kindness. As founder and president of Faith Hope and Love Community Inc., he demonstrates this belief by addressing food insecurity in Indianapolis. In this, IUPUI is Gonzales's perfect partner, considering the value the campus places on service, engagement, and community. Paws' Pantry, the university's student-created and student-run food pantry within the Division of Student Affairs, was a natural collaboration between Gonzales and the IUPUI campus.

After experiencing the pain of hunger firsthand while growing up in the Philippines, Gonzales was surprised to discover that food insecurity was also a critical issue in the

Merlin Gonzales. *Photo by Liz Kaye / Indiana University.*

Gonzales chats with former Paws' Pantry chair and fellow Face of IUPUI Michael Stottlemyer at the grand reopening of Paws' Pantry in 2018. *Photo by Liz Kaye / Indiana University.*

United States and even in Noblesville where he lives with his wife and two children. His answer was to develop food pantries designed to provide the at-risk population with food, supplies, and connections to resources within the community to establish long-term stability. That led Gonzales to Paws' Pantry, an all-volunteer operation that now partners with Faith Hope and Love for regular donations to stock its own shelves.

"I had the privilege of meeting cofounder Joe Spaulding when Paws' Pantry was getting ready to open in 2013," Gonzales said. "A few years later, Faith Hope and Love began providing fresh produce and other nonperishable food items to the pantry.

"I believe that a food pantry is needed in many colleges and universities," Gonzales explained. "Paws' Pantry is setting a new standard in our country. It is just a matter of time before more institutions follow this trend, and I am privileged to be a part of it. As Paws' Pantry grows, more students are open to using its services. Their dignity is preserved, and their quality of life is improved, directly and positively impacting their future."

Paws' Pantry, which moved into a new larger space within the Campus Center in the fall of 2018, is part of a network of organizations on campus that addresses food insecurity. The Campus Kitchen within the IUPUI Office of Sustainability rescues quality food that would have otherwise gone to waste from food services on campus. Campus Kitchen partners with Paws' Pantry to provide meals on campus as well as with organizations like Wheeler Mission to provide nutritious meals for clients in the Indianapolis community.

Merlin Gonzales and Faith Hope and Love are valuable partners in this vitally important effort to improve the lives of faculty, staff, and students at IUPUI and of people in the city of Indianapolis.

Lacy Johnson

Partner at Ice Miller, LLP; IUPUI Class of 1981, McKinney School of Law; Member, IUPUI Board of Advisors

IUPUI BOARD OF ADVISORS MEMBER LACY JOHNSON is a partner at Ice Miller LLP where he focuses his practice on public affairs and lobbying, sports, and entertainment, among other areas. A lifelong Hoosier, Johnson received his bachelor of arts degree in political science and industrial management from Purdue University and is a 1981 graduate of the Robert H. McKinney School of Law at IUPUI.

Outside of the office, Johnson is a well-known ambassador for the city of Indianapolis. As past president of the Indianapolis Airport Authority, he was instrumental in the

Lacy Johnson and his wife, Patricia, were both honored with the Cornerstone Award at the 2018 IU Partners in Philanthropy Ceremony. *Photo courtesy of IU Foundation.*

development of the new $1.3 billion Indianapolis International Airport. He serves on the board of directors for the Madam Walker Legacy Center and the American Pianists Association, and he is a former board member of Downtown Indy Inc.

As an active community servant, Johnson contributes his time and talent to a lengthy list of organizations, including the McKinney School of Law Board of Visitors, the Indiana University Foundation, Eskenazi Health, the Congressional Black Caucus Political Education and Leadership Institute, and the American Red Cross National Diversity Advisory Council, to name just a few. In all of this, Johnson exemplifies a spirit of service that far surpasses everyday expectations.

"It's my way of putting back some of what I've been given. I'm living the American dream. I've been touched by some fantastic people. What you can do with that is pass it on," Johnson said.

In recognition of all that he has achieved, Johnson received IU's highest alumni honor, the Distinguished Alumni Service Award, as well as a Sagamore of the Wabash Award from the state of Indiana.

In June 2018, Lacy and Patricia Johnson were honored with the IU Foundation's Partners in Philanthropy Cornerstone Award for their partnership, volunteerism, and generosity to philanthropic initiatives. In August 2018, the couple demonstrated their deeply rooted and focused commitment to diversity, and particularly to students of Color, with a $1.5 million gift to IU's Office of the Vice President for Diversity, Equity, and Multicultural Affairs to establish the Johnson Chair for Diversity and Leadership. The gift coincides with the establishment of the Black Philanthropy Circle, of which Lacy Johnson is a founding member.

The Johnsons have also supported underrepresented populations through Johnson Family Scholars in the Lilly Family School of Philanthropy and the Lacy M. Johnson Scholarship in the McKinney School of Law.

Facing Johnson accepts his Distinguished Alumni Service Award in 2014.
Photo courtesy of IU Foundation.

Alpha Blackburn
President and CEO of Blackburn Architects Inc.; Emeritus Member, IUPUI Board of Advisors

ALPHA BLACKBURN HAS BEEN A PILLAR of the Indianapolis community for more than four decades as an award-winning fashion designer and editor, a successful businesswoman and CEO, a civic leader, and a community volunteer, as well as a generous philanthropist. She is also a tireless advocate for the arts and a champion for education at IUPUI and beyond.

"I know the value of scholarships firsthand," Blackburn said. "I am the youngest in a family of eight, and I would not have attended college had I not won a national competitive scholarship to Howard University in our nation's capital. I graduated with a bachelor's degree in design and a master of fine arts degree in painting and art history."

In 2003, she established the Alpha Blackburn Scholarship for the Arts at Herron School of Art and Design at IUPUI to support and encourage young artists. Any

Alpha Blackburn (third from left) with past and present members of the IUPUI Board of Advisors, including fellow Face of IUPUI Ralph Taylor (far left). *Photo by Liz Kaye / Indiana University.*

IUPUI Chancellor Paydar presents Blackburn with her Chancellor's Medallion in 2017.
Photo by Liz Kaye / Indiana University.

full-time incoming freshman who is enrolled at Herron and exhibits outstanding creative talent is eligible, with special consideration given to students from underrepresented populations.

"I am an artist and a designer of both interiors and fashion, and my late husband, Walter, was an artist and architect," Blackburn said. "He designed Herron's original sculpture and ceramics facility on Indiana Avenue, now the Eskenazi Fine Arts Center. Walter actually took classes at Herron as a child. Funding a scholarship at Herron was a natural choice."

As a member of the Herron School of Art and Design Advisory Board, Blackburn has provided inspiration, guidance, and vision to its students, faculty, and staff. She has also served on the IUPUI Board of Advisors, and in 2017, Chancellor Paydar honored her with an IUPUI Chancellor's Medallion, the highest recognition the campus leader can bestow.

In addition to supporting Herron students with scholarships, Blackburn provides scholarship opportunities via the Walter Blackburn Scholarship Fund. Established in memory of her late husband, the scholarship provides four-year support for students pursuing architecture, fine art, performing arts, graphic arts, or design on any campus.

"I can attest that the gratification from having helped transform the lives of these young people is vastly disproportionate to such a small investment. I am convinced that our students will, like me, want to help the next generation of students, just as they were helped. Now that is a worthy legacy," Blackburn said.

Blackburn served as the fashion editor at *Indianapolis Monthly* from 1980 to 1990 and hosted daily and weekly local television talk shows from 1972 to 1981. She is the chairperson of the Indiana Civil Rights Commission, a position that she has held since 1987. She has also served on the board of the Indianapolis Symphony Society, the Key Bank Regional Board, the Indianapolis Cultural Development Commission, and the board of the Indianapolis Museum of Art.

Nina Mason Pulliam
Journalist

NINA MASON PULLIAM WAS A LIFELONG Hoosier whose last name was synonymous with newspaper publishing in Indianapolis for decades. A compassionate business and civic leader, Pulliam dedicated herself to serving and giving back to her community, a dedication that expresses itself at IUPUI through the Nina Mason Pulliam Legacy Scholars Program, established by the Nina Mason Pulliam Charitable Trust in 2001.

Born Nina Mason in rural Martinsville, Indiana, in 1906, she was just a teenager when she was first paid for a literary essay. This inspired her love for journalism, which she went on to study at Franklin College in Franklin, Indiana. She later attended Indiana University and the University of New Mexico before taking a full-time job at *Farm Life* magazine in Spencer, Indiana. When *Farm Life* ceased publication during the Depression, she went to work for an up-and-coming publisher named Eugene C. Pulliam, and they married in 1941.

The two made a publishing team, traveling extensively and chronicling the post–World War II conditions in Europe—the first Americans to do so. With stories published in newspapers across North America, Nina Mason Pulliam spent more than a decade pursuing her love of journalism, and her articles were collected in seven books. She advanced journalism as the founding secretary-treasurer and a director of Central Newspapers Inc., which Eugene Pulliam founded in 1934, and she served as president of CNI after he passed away in 1975 until 1979.

Pulliam was also one of the first women admitted to Sigma Delta Chi, now the Society of Professional Journalists. Groundbreaking in other ways as well, she became the first

Nina Mason Pulliam sits at her typewriter. *Photo courtesy of the Nina Mason Pulliam Charitable Trust.*

Pulliam was a trailblazer, including being the first woman to earn a private pilot's license in Indiana. *Photo courtesy of the Nina Mason Pulliam Charitable Trust.*

woman to earn a private pilot's license in Indiana.

Pulliam's legacy continues to impact and inspire the next generation of leaders through the Nina Scholars Program, which promotes and develops the success of underrepresented students from disadvantaged backgrounds. The program's holistic approach includes dedicated academic support, focused mentoring, career development, community service, and a scholarship toward the cost of attendance at IUPUI for up to six years. This program is one of only a handful of its kind in the country and adds eight new scholars each academic year. In April 2018, the Nina Mason Pulliam Charitable Trust established a $3 million endowment with the IU Foundation to support the Nina Mason Pulliam Legacy Scholars program in perpetuity.

"The impact of the Nina Scholars Program has been profound," said Rob McKibben, a mechanical engineering major and Nina Scholar. "Every aspect of my life has been enhanced by the practice of viewing challenges as opportunities to learn and grow. The way the curriculum is coupled with a supportive community of other students on similar journeys has made all the difference."

Pulliam passed away in 1997.

Ralph Taylor

Radio Color Analyst for Purdue University Men's Basketball; Member, IUPUI Board of Advisors

FANS OF BOILERMAKER BASKETBALL likely know the voice of Ralph Taylor. For the last thirteen seasons, he has been the radio color analyst for the Purdue University men's team. It is a fitting role for Taylor, a member of Purdue's 1969 Big Ten championship team that fell to UCLA in the NCAA championship during the Boilermakers' first Final Four appearance. In 1995, Taylor was selected as one of the top four all-time fan-favorite players in Purdue basketball history.

A gifted athlete who was inducted into the Indiana Basketball Hall of Fame in 2001, Taylor has also made a name for himself as a champion for diversity and inclusion in professional roles away from the microphone. As a former program officer for the Central Indiana Community Foundation, he launched the Sam H. Jones Creating Greater Awareness Forum to highlight the issues, challenges, and concerns facing Indianapolis's Asian, West Indian, Middle Eastern, American Indian, and Eastern European

Ralph Taylor (far left) with the broadcasting team for Purdue University men's basketball. *Photo courtesy of Ralph Taylor.*

communities. In addition, Taylor has served in the Indianapolis Mayor's Office of International and Cultural Affairs; was codirector of Welcoming Indianapolis; served as director of community service for the Indiana Youth Institute; and was an educator for the Purdue Cooperative Extension Service and Indianapolis Public Schools.

Taylor has also made a lasting local impact through his advocacy, volunteer work, and civic engagement. As a founding board member of the Immigrant Welcome Center in Indianapolis, he gives a voice to the city's newcomer communities by connecting them to resources critical to building a successful foundation. In 2010, he received the inaugural Diversity and Inclusion Champion Award from the YMCA of Greater Indianapolis for his work with the Chin Community of Indiana, Exodus Refugees Immigration Inc., and the African Center of Indianapolis, among others.

Taylor is past president of the Rotary Club of Indianapolis and the Indiana Basketball Hall of Fame Board of Directors. He currently serves on the IUPUI Board of Advisors and the Big Ten Commission, and he has previously served on the boards of the American Indian Center of Indiana, the Asian-American Alliance of Indiana, the United Way of Central Indiana Committee on Diversity, the IPS Education Foundation, the Indianapolis Arts Council, and Coburn Place.

Taylor received his bachelor's degree in health and kinesiology from Purdue University and has previously served on the Athletic Advisory Committee and the College of Health and Human Sciences Alumni Board at Purdue.

Taylor is a champion for diversity and inclusion away from the microphone. *Photo by Liz Kaye / Indiana University.*

Luis Franco

Mexican Consul in Indianapolis; Member, IUPUI Board of Advisors

IUPUI BOARD OF ADVISORS MEMBER LUIS FRANCO holds a unique and rare position: He represents the government of the only country in the world with a full-time consulate office in Indianapolis. As consul general of Mexico, Franco provides diplomatic leadership and advocacy to support the approximately four hundred thousand Mexican expatriates living in the region, which encompasses Indiana, Kentucky, and parts of Ohio and Illinois.

Above Mexican Consul General Luis Franco, Ivy Tech Community College Chancellor Kathleen Lee, and IUPUI Chancellor Paydar share a moment after signing a memorandum of understanding for the Station for Educational Orientation Program on February 28, 2019. *Photo by Liz Kaye / Indiana University.*

Facing As Mexican consul general, Franco provides invaluable services to the local community. *Photo by Liz Kaye / Indiana University.*

As Indianapolis becomes increasingly more diverse and the city's Latino communities continue to grow, with Latinos now accounting for about 6 percent of the total population, the services provided by the Mexican consulate are critically important for many. Acting as an extension of the Mexican embassy, the consulate provides a variety of administrative services and educational programs, from help obtaining passports and birth certificates to financial planning and workshops on relevant topics like labor rights.

In February 2019, IUPUI and the Mexican consulate in Indianapolis, along with Ivy Tech Community College, came together to sign a memorandum of understanding for the Ventanilla de Orientación Educativa (Station for Educational Orientation). Program, which is designed to create more educational opportunities for Mexican nationals in Central Indiana. Through the Office of Coordinated Programs, IUPUI provides information regarding admissions, scholarships, and financial aid, among other services, to potential students.

Franco was appointed head consul of Mexico in Indianapolis in 2017. Prior to that, he served as the Mexican consul in Salt Lake City. He was deputy chief of mission at the Mexican embassy in Sweden and deputy chief of mission and political affairs officer at the Mexican embassy in New Zealand.

He has received foreign civil awards and decorations from the governments of Argentina, Bolivia, Brazil, Chile, Estonia, France, Guatemala, Italy, Luxembourg, Paraguay, Portugal, Romania, South Korea, Spain, Sweden, Ukraine, and Venezuela.

Franco holds a bachelor's degree in international relations from Universidad Nacional Autónoma de México in Aragon, Mexico, and completed his postgraduate studies in international relations at the University of Florence in Italy. Franco has been a member of the Mexican Foreign Service since 1982.

James Taylor
President and CEO of John H. Boner Community Center; IUPUI Class of 1991, School of Social Work

FOR MORE THAN TWO DECADES, School of Social Work alumnus James Taylor has been a catalyst for the urban renewal and revitalization of Indianapolis's east side, connecting people to resources and each other. Under Taylor's leadership as chief executive officer since 1998, the John Boner Neighborhood Centers have helped generate millions of dollars in community development for the near-east side while also investing more than $56 million in a variety of initiatives to improve the quality of life for residents of the neighborhood.

Long recognized for civic engagement, IUPUI has partnered with Taylor and the John Boner Neighborhood Centers on a number of programs to advance their mission of creating a vibrant, thriving, welcoming community. Under Taylor's guidance and

James Taylor receives the 2018 Chancellor's Community Award for Excellence in Civic Engagement. *Photo by Liz Kaye / Indiana University.*

in collaboration with IUPUI, among other partners, the John Boner Neighborhood Centers developed a grassroots quality-of-life plan for the near-east side in 2006. Ultimately, this quality-of-life plan was used to establish and leverage a partnership with the 2012 Indianapolis Super Bowl Host Committee, from which the Near Eastside Legacy Project was born.

One component of the legacy project is the Boner Fitness and Learning Center, which opened in February 2012, offering a holistic menu of targeted educational and wellness services for neighborhood children, families, and seniors. The facility, an extension of the John Boner Neighborhood Centers and the result of Taylor's vision, features a state-of-the-art media studio, mobile computer lab, educational greenhouse and garden, instructional kitchen, art studio, and full-service fitness facility staffed by students from IUPUI's School of Health & Human Sciences.

In 2015, IUPUI collaborated again with Taylor and the John Boner Neighborhood Centers, along with the Eskenazi Health Center, Ivy Tech Community College, Crispus Attucks High School, and the Rehabilitation Hospital of Indiana, to develop and implement the Indiana University Health Careers Opportunity Program. The initiative aims to diversify the health care workforce via a comprehensive community approach that provides disadvantaged students with the academic tools and social skills needed to graduate from health professions programs.

IUPUI Vice Chancellor for Community Engagement Amy Conrad Warner said, "James has been the single most successful, entrepreneurial, and inclusive community partner in Indianapolis for the past twenty-five years. He has championed the development of the near-east side neighborhood, partnered with IUPUI on the Boner Fitness and Learning Center and the Health Careers Opportunity Program, and established the federal designation for the Indy East Promise Zone. His aspirational civic leadership in Indianapolis is a shining example of what it means to be an IUPUI alum."

Taylor received the 2016 Michael A. Carroll Leadership Award and the 2018 Chancellor's Community Award for Excellence in Civic Engagement for his unwavering commitment to Indianapolis's eastside neighborhoods and his tireless dedication to uplifting those who call it home.

Facing Taylor has been a catalyst for the urban renewal of Indianapolis's east side.
Photo by Liz Kaye / Indiana University.

Above Hundreds of IUPUI faculty, staff, and students participated in a 50th anniversary campus-sponsored Habitat for Humanity build. The Peppers family assisted with the construction of the near westside construction and received their keys on December 12, 2018. *Photo by Liz Kaye / Indiana University.*

Facing top Third-grade students from Indianapolis Public Schools enjoy an IUPUI men's basketball game on January 24, 2019, at the Indiana Farmers Coliseum. *Photo courtesy of IUPUI Athletics.*

Facing bottom Chancellor Paydar honored all five living mayors of Indianapolis with Chancellor's Medallions at his 2019 Report to the Community. *Photo by Liz Kaye / Indiana University.*

Following page On November 14, 2018, IUPUI hosted its second naturalization ceremony in partnership with the US District Court for the Southern District of Indiana. One hundred men and women from twenty-seven countries became new United States citizens that day. *Photo by Liz Kaye / Indiana University.*

3. ANTICIPATING OUR FUTURE
IUPUI Alumni Change the Campus, the Circle City, and Beyond

SINCE 1969, MORE THAN 210,000 STUDENTS have graduated from IUPUI. The scope and scale of their impact is impossible to measure. One student of dentistry returned to her home in Thailand and became dentist to the king there. A graduate in social work has served as an advisor on homeland security to US presidents. Still others have served at the highest levels of the US government. IUPUI-trained teachers, nurses, therapists, artists, lawyers, engineers, policymakers, historians, and many others have shaped their careers around building a better future for humanity.

These Faces of IUPUI—and the other IUPUI alumni throughout this volume—reflect the nearly limitless windows of opportunity their degrees opened for IUPUI graduates and the tremendous contributions they have made to the campus and to the world.

Above Jaguars at Regatta during IUPUI's fortieth-anniversary take to the Indianapolis Central Canal. *Photo courtesy of IU Alumni Association.*

Facing A precursor to today's Regatta, this raft race shows IUPUI students on the move (undated). *Photo courtesy of IUPUI Special Collections and Archives (UA24–005129s).*

SPOTLIGHT ON IUPUI HISTORY

The roots of IUPUI Regatta

Nate Mugg

Lead Creative Designer, IUPUI Multimedia Production Center; IUPUI Class of 2006, School of Engineering and Technology, and Class of 2017, School of Liberal Arts

AS THE LEAD CREATIVE DESIGNER at the Multimedia Production Center, Nate Mugg puts his artistic talents to work to support the programs of the Division of Student Affairs and IUPUI student organizations. Evidence of his creative touches and those of his talented team of student designers can be seen all around campus, around Indianapolis, and around the world.

"Nate has played a pivotal role in the success of the Division of Student Affairs's new marketing campaign. He has a wonderful work ethic and great attention to detail," said Dr. Eric Weldy, vice chancellor for student affairs. "One of the things I like most about Nate is that he goes out of his way to support his student employees. He gives them great hands-on experience and provides a very healthy working environment for them to thrive."

As an undergraduate student at IUPUI, Mugg was studying computer graphics technology when he was hired at the MPC in 2005 as a student designer. In addition to working there, he held several different jobs within the Division of Student Affairs: resident assistant, information desk staff, and secretary of Undergraduate Student Government.

"I like that I can take my skills in design and use them to promote the vast array of programs that students can benefit from, just as I did," said Mugg. "Coming from those roles, I see the value in all of the services the Division of Student Affairs offers to students. I hope my impact helps students learn about, and take advantage of, all the great programs the division offers while I also serve as a good mentor to the students who work in my area day to day."

By his own admission, Mugg's collegiate journey was a little roundabout. After a few semesters in pre-med biology and then a couple of years studying nursing, he decided to turn his graphic design hobby into a career. He began his full-time job at the MPC after graduating from the School of Engineering and Technology. Ten years later, he completed his bachelor's degree in general studies at IUPUI.

Facing Nate Mugg. *Photo by Liz Kaye / Indiana University.*

Mugg meets with some of his 2018 Multimedia Production Center student employees. *Photo by Liz Kaye / Indiana University.*

"I would say that finishing my bachelor's degree is for sure my top accomplishment because once I got my job at IUPUI with my associate degree, I put my studies on hold. I eventually got married and had kids, and it wasn't until my former supervisor, Andrea Anderson, pushed me to finish my degree that I finally completed everything. Experiencing that kind of support was great," Mugg said.

Both as a student and as a professional, Mugg has been a member of the IUPUI campus community for a combined eighteen years, and he has created quite a collection of fond memories. "The one thing that ties all those memories together, though, are the people I've gotten to know and become friends with over the years and the relationships that I have formed," he said.

Taylor Rhodes

Corporate Volunteerism Coordinator, United Way of Central Indiana; IUPUI Class of 2012, School of Liberal Arts, and Class of 2018, Paul H. O'Neill School of Public and Environmental Affairs and Lilly Family School of Philanthropy

Two-time IUPUI alumna Rhodes has already earned her place in IUPUI history. She is a two-time recipient of the Plater Civic Engagement Medallion, both as an undergraduate and as a graduate student, for her outstanding commitment to community service. She shares this distinction with just one other graduate. Locally and even globally, Rhodes's impact is undeniable.

From left: Rhodes's older sister Jordan, her friend Kiran Gill, founding Dean Emerita of the Honors College E. Jane Luzar, Rhodes's younger sister Morgan, and Taylor Rhodes in 2011. *Photo courtesy of Taylor Rhodes.*

Taylor Rhodes has been honored twice with a Plater Civic Engagement Medallion.
Photo by Liz Kaye / Indiana University.

"I think the Plater Medallion, out of all the different accolades, means the most because it really speaks to what you have done with your time as a student, how you have gone above and beyond just being in the classroom, trying to do things for your community and society as a whole," said Rhodes.

A look at her list of academic accomplishments and campus and civic contributions quickly reveals why she has been honored twice. As an undergraduate, she was actively involved with the IUPUI Student Foundation and Jagathon, IUPUI's Dance Marathon; she served as a 21st Century Scholars peer mentor; and she studied abroad in Denmark where she learned about corporate social responsibility.

After Rhodes received her bachelor's degree in international studies from the School of Liberal Arts in 2012, she spent two years mentoring and coaching underserved middle school students in Washington, DC, through the City Year AmeriCorps Program.

In 2014, she returned to IUPUI and enrolled in the dual degree master's program with the O'Neill School of Public and Environmental Affairs and the Lilly Family School of Philanthropy. Rhodes completed her master of arts in philanthropic studies and master of public administration in nonprofit management in August 2018.

During her master's work, she was president of Graduate and Professional Student Government, worked extensively with Paws' Pantry through the Office of Student Advocacy and Support, and traveled to Uganda for an eleven-week internship where she worked with primary schools on sustainable development.

"I had a lot of different opportunities, both as an undergraduate and as a grad student. I studied abroad in really unique places in unique programs. I had the time of my life, and I learned a lot culturally and about myself," Rhodes said. "I've also had leadership opportunities I don't think I would have had at other universities. I've been part of so many student organizations and events, and that's helped me strengthen my leadership skills."

Currently, Rhodes is launching her career in philanthropy as the corporate volunteerism coordinator for United Way of Central Indiana. A passionate supporter of United Way and its mission, she is excited every day to be able to give back to the Indianapolis community.

"Something I learned in City Year and I've taken with me is *ubuntu*," she said. "It's a Swahili philosophy that basically means 'my humanity is tied to yours.' To me, community service is something you should do, something you have to do, to make everyone great. To make yourself great, the whole community has to be great," said Rhodes.

Mariana Lopez-Owens

Director of Community Engagement and Events, La Plaza; IUPUI Class of 2014, School of Liberal Arts

IUPUI ALUMNA MARIANA LOPEZ-OWENS is living her American dream. Lopez-Owens graduated in 2014 from the School of Liberal Arts at IUPUI with a bachelor's degree in Spanish and global and international studies. In 2017, she received her master's degree in public affairs from the O'Neill School of Public and Environmental Affairs at Indiana University Bloomington. Shortly thereafter, she returned to IUPUI to join the staff of the Richard M. Fairbanks School of Public Health.

"As a first-generation, low-income student, attending IUPUI was life-changing. Had it not been for all of the opportunities afforded to me at IUPUI, I wouldn't have had the support I needed to achieve my dreams," said Lopez-Owens.

Her path toward Indiana and IUPUI began more than 1,700 miles from Indianapolis. In 1999, when she was seven years old, Lopez-Owens and her family embarked on a journey that would alter the course of her life—their lives—forever when they left their home country of Mexico for the United States and the promise of a better life. The family entered the United States in January 2000 and eventually put down roots in Indianapolis.

"Our mother continues to instill values tied closely to resilience and innovative solutions," said Lopez-Owens. "She silences anyone who says something can't be done and supports us by allowing us room to pursue any dream we have."

Another critical turning point came when Lopez-Owens and her sisters were adopted by her stepfather, which led to their US citizenship. After her graduation from North Central High School, scholarships helped launch her collegiate career at IUPUI where she joined her older sister, who is now also an IUPUI alumna.

While a student at IUPUI, Lopez-Owens made significant contributions inside and outside of the classroom. In addition to her dual major and double minors—in Latino studies and sociology—she was a member of the Jaguars track and field and cross-country teams. She served as president of the Latino Student Association and on the Student-Athlete Advisory Committee.

Facing Mariana Lopez-Owens in the Fairbanks School of Public Health.
Photo by Liz Kaye / Indiana University.

Lopez-Owens (center) with Chancellor Emeritus Charles R. Bantz and Most Outstanding Male Student Ben Judge when she was awarded Most Outstanding Female Student in 2014.
Photo courtesy of Mariana Lopez-Owens.

At the Top 100 program in 2014, Lopez-Owens was named IUPUI's Most Outstanding Female Student in recognition of her academic achievements, campus engagement, and civic and community service. The following year, she received the William M. Plater Civic Engagement Medallion for her above-and-beyond commitment to the community as an IUPUI student.

"The extraordinary faculty and staff nurtured my talents and worked selflessly to allow me to succeed," she said. "I was afforded the opportunity to have the finest of higher education experiences at IUPUI."

With this support, she has continued progressing in her career and currently serves as director of community engagement and events at La Plaza, an Indianapolis nonprofit focused on the academic success of Latino youth as well as preparing families for success in the workforce and the community. Lopez-Owens is also an English as a second language instructional assistant and an active volunteer at the Immigrant Welcome Center.

André Zhang Sonera

Special Assistant to the Mayor of Indianapolis; IUPUI Class of 2016 and Class of 2020, Paul H. O'Neill School of Public and Environmental Affairs

COMING FROM THE SMALL TOWN OF San Sebastián in Puerto Rico, André Zhang Sonera never dreamed he would have the opportunity to go to college on the mainland, much less graduate from the Paul H. O'Neill School of Public and Environmental Affairs at IUPUI. A chance encounter and quick conversation about IUPUI at the National FFA Organization convention in Indianapolis in 2010 changed that. A follow-up phone call with an IUPUI admissions advisor allowed Zhang Sonera to begin imagining himself as a Jaguar.

"The most appealing factor of this campus for me was its proximity and integration with downtown Indianapolis and the different partnerships and collaborations with

André Zhang Sonera with Indianapolis Mayor Joe Hogsett. *Photo courtesy of André Zhang Sonera.*

Zhang Sonera (third row, eleventh from right) with White House interns and President of the United States Barack Obama (center). *Photo courtesy of André Zhang Sonera.*

the many community organizations and entities that serve its residents," Zhang Sonera said.

Passionate about public service and civic engagement, Zhang Sonera majored in civic leadership and minored in policy studies, earning his bachelor of arts in 2016. During his sophomore year, he participated in the Sam H. Jones Community Service Scholarship Program, which more firmly rooted his civic-minded future.

Three internships during his undergraduate years exposed Zhang Sonera to a possible career in public service. In 2014, during the fall semester of his junior year, he served as an intern for the Executive Office of the President at the White House through the O'Neill School's Washington Leadership Program. The following summer, as an operations intern in the City of New York Mayor's Office of Operations, he evaluated the quality and availability of interpretation services for residents with limited English proficiency. In the fall of 2015, he coordinated logistics and event management as an intern for the Indiana Bicentennial Commission in the Office of the Lieutenant Governor.

At the same time, Zhang Sonera was deeply engaged on and around campus. He worked with the Office of Undergraduate Admissions to help recruit Latino students to IUPUI, served as a resident assistant in student housing, organized alternative spring break trips to Trinidad and Tobago, and joined the IUPUI Martin Luther King Jr. Day of Service. He was also an active community servant, volunteering his time and talent at Ronald McDonald House of Indiana and United Way of Central Indiana.

In 2016, during his first year as a graduate student in the O'Neill School, Zhang Sonera was selected as the inaugural Peterson Fellow through a program established by former Indianapolis Mayor Bart Peterson to provide an immersive one-year paid internship for an O'Neill School graduate student with a career interest in public service. That fellowship translated into a more permanent role for Zhang Sonera, who is pursuing his master's in public affairs while serving as special assistant to Indianapolis Mayor Joe Hogsett.

Kathleen Hursh, O'Neill School associate director of career development, said, "It has been an honor to work with André throughout his undergraduate and graduate career here at IUPUI. He has taken full advantage of the many opportunities available at the O'Neill School and is a wonderful example of an engaged alumnus. He is an active member on our alumni panels, making time to speak with students about internship opportunities and about the challenges of entering the workforce."

"I am who I am today because I am a Jaguar, and for that, I am eternally grateful," Zhang Sonera said.

Priya Dave
IUPUI Class of 2018, School of Liberal Arts

"My time at IUPUI was transformational. The many opportunities I was afforded not only provided me a solid foundation for medical school but also instilled in me life-long passions and scholarly interests," said IUPUI Top 100 Most Outstanding Student and 2018 graduate Priya Dave.

A graduate of Center Grove High School in Greenwood, Indiana, Dave was drawn to the IUPUI School of Liberal Arts Medical Humanities and Health Studies Program, which focuses on the social, economic, and cultural contexts of health and how human

Above Priya Dave (center right) with colleagues in the University of Havana Distributed Drug Discovery Lab. *Photo courtesy of Priya Dave.*

Facing Dave speaks at the Top 100 Undergraduates Recognition Ceremony.
Photo courtesy of IUPUI Alumni Relations.

beings relate to health, illness, and death. The program gave her the opportunity to explore the many fields and professions that connect medicine and liberal arts.

"I was a biology major when I started college, but then I took a medical humanities class and really loved it. It was an opportunity to explore something completely different that I wouldn't have had time to do while in medical school. This major was a perfect fit for me," Dave said.

Dave knew medical school was in her future as a child watching her younger sister battle a chronic illness. "Seeing the doctor-patient relationship during her visits helped confirm the career I wanted," said Dave, now a medical student at the Icahn School of Medicine at Mount Sinai in New York City.

At IUPUI, Dave sought out experiences that allowed her to apply her interests in medical humanities to real-world situations. As a freshman, she traveled to the Dominican Republic with Timmy Global Health to help set up a medical clinic in a rural community there. Later, she traveled to Cuba with the School of Science's Department of Chemistry and Chemical Biology. There, at the University of Havana, she served as a teaching assistant in the Distributed Drug Discovery Lab, a global collaboration to educate students in chemistry and biology while seeking treatments for neglected diseases. She also traveled to Nicaragua and Panama to volunteer with Global Medical Brigades.

Also as an undergraduate, Dave served as a campus ambassador, leading tours for prospective students and representing IUPUI at a variety of community events. Along with being selected as the top undergraduate student at IUPUI in 2018, she was also the School of Liberal Arts Faculty Medal of Distinction recipient, a William M. Plater Civic Engagement Medallion honoree, and a Bepko Scholar.

"IUPUI provided the ideal environment to excel in anything and everything I could imagine. The city of Indianapolis and my mentors, instructors, and peers at this university have been monumental in achieving my dreams," said Dave.

Ali Emswiller

IUPUI Class of 2018, School of Health & Human Sciences, and Class of 2021 (expected), O'Neill School of Public and Environmental Affairs

To say that 2018 alumna and graduate student Ali Emswiller has made a difference at IUPUI is a huge understatement. To say that she is an incredible inspiration to fellow students, faculty, and staff more accurately captures the remarkable impact she has had on others, including the patients and their families at Riley Hospital for Children as president of Jagathon, IUPUI's Dance Marathon.

In 2018, while Ali was president, Jagathon raised $501,371 for pediatric research at Riley Hospital. This is the third consecutive year that the university's largest student-run philanthropic organization set a new fund-raising record. The impact that Jagathon has had on Emswiller is equally profound.

"It is truly because of Jagathon that I am pursuing a master of public affairs in non-profit management in the O'Neill School and a career in philanthropic fund-raising.

Ali Emswiller makes an announcement at the 2018 Jagathon. *Photo by Liz Kaye / Indiana University.*

Jagathon has helped me realize my true passion and talents for philanthropy, and I intend to continue my involvement on campus as long as I can," said Emswiller, who served as vice president of finance for Jagathon in the 2018–2019 academic year.

In 2015, Emswiller attended Jagathon as a freshman, a new college student trying to find her way. By the end of the marathon, she was hooked. She joined the organizing committee the following week, and a few months later, she assumed the role of director of special events on the executive board.

Pete Hunter, director of development at IUPUI for the Indiana University Foundation, said, "Jagathon experienced unprece-dented growth during Ali's tenure. The program raised about six times more in 2019 than it did in 2015, and no one has been more instrumental in this growth than Ali. She is the only student in the program's eighteen-year history to serve four years on the executive board. During that time, she has done so much to develop Jagathon into a nationally relevant program and among the fastest-growing student-led philanthropies in the country. It is personally fulfilling knowing that, as such an incredibly talented and hard-working individual, Ali is dedicated to improving her community."

Not only did the 2018 Jagathon break fund-raising records, it also included the largest student registration in the event's history, with 1,362 participants. Part of the IUPUI Student Foundation, Jagathon has received multiple awards from the Children's Miracle Network, including the 2017 Miracle Maker Award, and in 2018, the Partner-ship Award and the Organization Management Award.

"I am deeply inspired by the passion that IUPUI has for philan-thropy, particularly for Riley Hospital for Children since it is located on the IUPUI campus. The experience of being surrounded by people who work year-round to give so much of themselves to support others keeps me going. My involvement with Jagathon has given me so much pride in my campus that I know I will carry it with me forever," said Emswiller.

Emswiller is the only student in Jagathon history to serve on the executive board for four years, and she continues her engagement as a graduate assistant with the IU Foundation. *Photo by Liz Kaye / Indiana University.*

Jordan Nelsen

IUPUI Class of 2018, Herron School of Art and Design and School of Informatics and Computing

SINCE SHE WAS A LITTLE GIRL CARRYING a sketch pad and a pencil, 2018 IUPUI alumna Jordan Nelsen knew that she wanted to be an artist. As a student in the Herron School of Art and Design and the School of Informatics and Computing, Nelsen's artistic tools and techniques evolved to include the use of a stylus instead of a pencil, digital sculpting techniques and 3-D design, and scanning and printing expertise, skills that she has put to use in unique and life-changing ways.

While working toward her bachelor of science degree in media arts and science, Nelsen became involved in facial prosthetic reconstruction research, collaborating for two years with prosthodontic resident Dr. Travis Bellicchi in the School of Dentistry

Above Jordan Nelsen works on a design. *Photo by Ann Marie Shambaugh. Reused by permission. Copyright 2019. Current Publishing, LLC. All rights reserved.*

Facing Nelsen has put her design skills to use in life-changing ways. *Photo courtesy of Jordan Nelsen.*

to create facial prostheses for patients who had lost features due to cancer, burns, and congenital disorders. During that time, Nelsen played a critical role in twenty-three patient cases, including one for which she digitally designed a prosthesis in less than four hours, which led to an unprecedented device delivery time of less than twenty-four hours.

"I have always been very interested in both anatomy and art. Finding a niche that satisfies both of those interests while also being able to directly impact people has been a dream come true," Nelsen said. "I've had the opportunity to work on a variety of patient cases, one of them involving the creation of a dental surgical guide that was the first of its kind in dentistry and in the world. I have been truly humbled by the work I've been able to be a part of."

"The level of commitment and professionalism that Jordan demonstrates is outstanding. She is an extraordinary artist," said Bellicchi. "Still, what makes her truly special is her work ethic. I am so thankful we had the opportunity to work together. I look forward to further collaboration with her."

Nelsen also spent two years working with IU School of Medicine Professor Of Neurological Surgery Dr. Aaron Cohen-Gadol to complete 3-D medical visualizations for his Neurosurgical Atlas, an internationally renowned educational tool for the sharing and advancement of neurosurgical techniques.

In 2018, Nelsen was not only recognized as a Top 100 Outstanding Student but was also selected to the Top 10 Outstanding Students for her academic achievements, campus involvement, and community service. Since graduation, Nelsen has launched her career as an illustrator and has continued to explore her medical work using emerging technologies such as augmented reality and virtual reality.

Facing top The IUPUI Top 100 Undergraduate Recognition Ceremony includes special recognition for the top ten students as well as the top student overall as judged by their academic performance, campus leadership, and community engagement. Here, the top eleven students strike their favorite poses with Chancellor Paydar. *Photo by John Gentry.*

Facing bottom The 2019 fund-raising record for Jagathon, IUPUI's Dance Marathon, supporting pediatric research at Riley Hospital for Children, surpassed the previous year's total by more than $100,000. *Photo courtesy of News at IU.*

TOP 100
A LIFETIME of SUCCESS

TOP 100
A LIFETIME of SUCCESS

IUPUI

100

TOP 100
A LIFETIME of SUCCESS

TOP 100
A LIFETIME of SUCCESS

TOP

SPOTLIGHT ON THE 50TH ANNIVERSARY

A springtime of celebration at IUPUI

dance

$ 6 0 5 , 1 7 8 . 2 4

on

IUPUI celebrates its top fifty graduate students with an Elite 50 Ceremony, hosted by Graduate and Professional Student Government and the Division of Student Affairs. The 2019 honorees pose here with Chancellor Paydar. *Photo by Liz Kaye / Indiana University.*

Anticipating Our Future: IUPUI 50th Anniversary Class of 2019

On Saturday, May 11, at Lucas Oil Stadium in downtown Indianapolis, IUPUI celebrated the Class of 2019. The campus awarded 7,899 degrees and certificates to 7,105 students: among others, 811 doctoral degrees, 1,750 master's degrees, 4,241 bachelor's degrees, and 69 associate's degrees. This includes IUPUI's Indiana University and Purdue University graduates.

Of the more than 7,000 graduates, 6,036 were Hoosiers, and nearly a quarter of the undergraduates were first-generation students, like several of the Faces of IUPUI included in this volume. The oldest graduate in the Class of 2019 was seventy-four, and the youngest was nineteen. In addition, the Class of 2019 included seven sets of twins.

While one can perform these calculations regarding the Class of 2019, their character is more difficult to measure and quantify. Faces of IUPUI 2019 graduates studied education, robotics, health informatics, environmental health science, fine art, and music. They served as peer mentors, represented IUPUI in NCAA Division I sports, and led campus efforts to address food insecurity. These Faces hail from India, Saudi Arabia, and the United States, bringing diverse perspectives to bear and making an impact at IUPUI that suggests the inspiring ways they will put their degrees to work in the years to come.

The Faces of IUPUI that follow offer a snapshot of the Class of 2019 as a whole. They are the leaders of tomorrow and are taking the IUPUI spirit around the world.

Following page The first IUPUI commencement ceremony was held at the Indiana State Fairgrounds Coliseum on June 9, 1970. The ceremony marked the third time that Purdue University had awarded undergraduate degrees in Indianapolis and the first time that Indiana University had done so. *Photo courtesy of IUPUI Special Collections and Archives (UA024_002413).*

Abdullah Alzeer
IUPUI Class of 2019, School of Informatics and Computing

When international doctoral student Abdullah Alzeer came to IUPUI in 2012, he did so with two goals in mind: obtain his PhD in health informatics from the School of Informatics and Computing and serve the Saudi community in Indianapolis while doing so. Propelled by his own experience working with a team to create a Saudi student club at Northern Kentucky University while obtaining his master's degree, Alzeer turned the then-defunct IUPUI Saudi Students Club into an award-winning model for a successful student organization.

"The first thing I did when I came to IUPUI was look to serve the Saudi community in Indianapolis through the Saudi Club at IUPUI. I worked with the Office of International Affairs and other Saudi community members at IUPUI to revive the club," Alzeer said. "Once the organization was reactivated, my first official role was serving as the media secretary in 2012, which allowed me to work closely with several departments at IUPUI and organizations in Indianapolis."

In 2016, while also serving as an adjunct lecturer in the Department of BioHealth Informatics, Alzeer stepped into the club's top position as president. During his tenure, the club hosted more than one hundred events focused on academics, community service, personal development, social interactions, and cultural outreach. Under Alzeer's leadership, the club created an Al-Majlis, or Saudi clubhouse, which promotes fellowship between and among IUPUI's Saudi population and the community. It also hosted Artal, an event dedicated to volunteering, for more than 350 Saudi clubs and organizations around the country, featuring speaker presentations and poster sessions that showcased the importance of volunteerism and philanthropy. Another key accomplishment was the publication of the *Arabic Academic Guide*, a lengthy guidebook written in Arabic and designed to help Arabic-speaking international students transition to the university and succeed academically.

Sandra Lemons, former director of international student services at IUPUI, said, "Abdullah is unlike many PhD students I know in that he managed to excel in his academic program while at the same time dedicating an enormous amount of time and effort to other meaningful activities. He got involved on campus and in the community the day he started his program. Abdullah has a passion for community service, and

Facing Abdullah Alzeer. *Photo by Liz Kaye / Indiana University.*

Alzeer (center) accepts the IUPUI Saudi Students Club's award for being the nation's top Saudi college student organization from the Saudi Arabian Cultural Mission to the USA in 2017. *Photo courtesy of News at IU.*

during his tenure as an SSC leader, he encouraged and expanded Saudi student service in Indianapolis."

The culmination of Alzeer's involvement with the IUPUI SSC came in November 2017, when the club was honored by the Saudi Arabian Cultural Mission as the top Saudi student club in the United States, among hundreds of other candidates. The deciding factors in this award included commitment to community service and initiating positive change. This tremendous honor and achievement also raised the profile of IUPUI in the Middle East.

"Some might say my biggest achievement was finishing my PhD at a respected university in the United States. Others could say it was leading the SSC to be the number-one Saudi club over the other three hundred clubs in the country. Personally, I think my biggest accomplishment is my six years of continuous community service and engagement. Nothing is more rewarding than receiving an unexpected email or text from one of the SSC members telling me how the club and our work impacted or made a difference to them," said Alzeer.

Abby Boatman

IUPUI Class of 2019, Fairbanks School of Public Health; Jaguar Volleyball Player

A FOUR-YEAR STUDENT-ATHLETE AND NATIVE of Bloomington, Indiana, Abby Boatman is one tough Jaguar as the middle blocker on the IUPUI volleyball team, with the records and honors to prove it. In the classroom, she is a dedicated student who is continuing her studies in dental school now that she has graduated from IUPUI with a degree in environmental health science from the Richard M. Fairbanks School of Public Health. On campus and in the community, Boatman raised engagement to a new level.

Abby Boatman spikes the ball during a volleyball game. *Photo courtesy of IUPUI Athletics.*

Boatman was one of the Summit League's top defensive players and was named to the 2017 Horizon League Academic All-Conference Team. *Photo courtesy of IUPUI Athletics.*

"Of all the universities I looked at during my volleyball recruiting process, I felt that IUPUI would best position me to reach my goals. As a student-athlete, I was intrigued by all of the academic and athletic opportunities available here," said Boatman.

Boatman emerged as one of the Summit League's top defensive players during her sophomore year and was twice named the league's Defensive Player of the Week before IUPUI switched to the Horizon League in 2017. As a junior, Boatman recorded a team-high 142 total blocks, the second-highest single-season mark in IUPUI history. She started each of the team's thirty-one matches, helping them to a 12–4 record in their first season of Horizon League play. That year, she was named to the 2017 Horizon League Academic All-Conference Team.

While she was shining on the volleyball court, Boatman also excelled in the classroom. She was a seven-time Academic Advisor's List honoree and consistently made the Fairbanks School of Public Health's Dean's List for a 3.5 grade point average or better. She was awarded the Michael A. Carroll Scholarship for the 2018–2019 academic year, which recognizes one IUPUI student-athlete per year for his or her commitment to community service as well as academic and athletic achievements. She was also honored as a 50th Anniversary Top 100 Outstanding Student.

"Looking back at my four years, the qualities of IUPUI that attracted me to the school held true. My time at IUPUI not only met my expectations but exceeded them," Boatman said.

In addition to her dedication in the classroom and on the court, Boatman was able to balance on-campus volunteer positions as well as community service activities. She served as president of the Fairbanks School of Public Health Undergraduate Association and as president of the IUPUI Pre-Dental Club, and she was a Bepko Learning Center mentor. She was actively involved with the Jags Reading Club and Paws' Pantry, and she represented the volleyball program in the Colts Change the Play Program partnership with Riley Hospital for Children.

"Abby is one of the most involved student-athletes I've ever had the pleasure of coaching. She was the recipient of the team ROAR Award in two seasons for being an outstanding representative of our program culture: in the gym, on campus, and in the community. As a team captain, she brought a lot of positive energy and took the time to connect with her teammates. I'm still impressed with all the clubs and campus activities she was a part of while also competing and maintaining a competitive GPA. She is a great example for future student-athletes who want to maximize their college experience and prepare for life after collegiate sports," said Lindsey Buteyn, IUPUI women's head volleyball coach.

Zach Carrico
IUPUI Class of 2019, Herron School of Art and Design

PHOTOGRAPHY AND ART HISTORY STUDENT Zach Carrico's college career culminated in May 2019 with a bachelor of fine arts degree from Herron School of Art and Design. Carrico, a native of Lafayette, Indiana, uses art and imagery as a way to express queer identity and the political climate around the LGBTQ+ community.

"I chose IUPUI because I felt that the environment would encourage me to understand my identity more and allow my identity to impact my academics, and vice versa. Creating photography that speaks to my nonbinary gender identity and sharing that with a class of my peers is so validating," said Carrico.

Outside of coursework, Carrico took a love of photography and art and applied it at the IUPUI Campus Center's Cultural Arts Gallery as a gallery assistant. Starting in the gallery in 2015, Carrico worked there while an undergraduate, also serving as the gallery photographer and promotions manager.

In addition to working behind the scenes, Carrico has had photography showcased in a number of venues. In November 2017, the Cultural Arts Gallery's *Military Tattoos @ IUPUI* exhibition featured images of thirty IUPUI veterans taken by Carrico and fellow student Shelby Flora. Last fall, Carrico's photograph titled "pansies" appeared in IUPUI's *genesis* literature and art magazine, which has been publishing the outstanding creative work of IUPUI students since 1972.

"At IUPUI, I was able to grow and develop my identity and also mature within my photography and artwork to articulate what queer identity means to me," said Carrico.

Carrico plans to pursue a future in fashion photography.

Facing top Zach Carrico. *Photo by Liz Kaye / Indiana University.*

Facing bottom Carrico works on a project in the photography dark room at the Herron School of Art and Design. *Photo by Liz Kaye / Indiana University.*

Breon Johnson
IUPUI Class of 2019, School of Liberal Arts

BREON JOHNSON, AN IUPUI GRADUATE from the School of Liberal Arts, hails from the southeast side of Fort Wayne, Indiana, but IUPUI is his home. Upon his arrival at IUPUI, Johnson immersed himself in the campus community, taking advantage of the many opportunities to get involved and stay engaged, including performing on the IUPUI Talent Stage during the 50th Anniversary Fall Kickoff Celebration in August 2019.

"My favorite part about being an IUPUI student is the community. There are so many places and spaces around campus that really help foster and build a strong sense of community, and I think those places are necessary for students to be successful and able to thrive," Johnson said.

A first-generation college student, Johnson graduated in May 2019 with a general studies degree, a minor in music, and a certificate in health administration. During his

Breon Johnson. *Photo by Liz Kaye / Indiana University.*

Johnson was the featured singer at the 2019 IUPUI Celebration of Black Graduates, performing the Black National Anthem, "Lift Ev'ry Voice and Sing." *Photo courtesy of GradPhotos.*

collegiate career, he served in more than a dozen different roles on and around campus. Those positions included—but were certainly not limited to—outreach ambassador for underrepresented populations in the Study Abroad Office, leadership positions within the Black Student Union, mentor for the Diversity Enrichment and Achievement Program, and peer educator for the IUPUI Multicultural Center where he promoted social justice education through dialogue and student-led workshops.

Dennis Rudnick, former associate director of multicultural education and research in the Division of Diversity, Equity, and Inclusion at IUPUI, said, "Breon is just a remarkable human being. In his role as a multicultural peer educator, he helped transform IUPUI for the better. He is thoughtful, compassionate, and steadfast in his commitment to social change through education. His leadership impact will resonate on this campus for generations."

Johnson plans to pursue a master's degree in higher education and student affairs. Ultimately, he hopes to put his academic, professional, and leadership experience to work in a university setting to advocate for, support, and develop policies and initiatives that create and strengthen the climate for success for college students.

Michael Stottlemyer
IUPUI Class of 2019, School of Science

IN HIS YEARS AT IUPUI, SECONDARY math education major Michael Stottlemyer made significant contributions to campus, contributions that by all accounts promise to have a lasting impact.

Countless examples illustrate Stottlemyer's outspoken advocacy for others, including his testimony as a freshman at the Indiana Statehouse in support of student scholarships, his guidance to local high school students both as a tutor and as a teaching assistant, and his outstanding leadership at Paws' Pantry that stimulated its growth and expansion.

"I have always wanted to speak up for what's right," said Stottlemyer, who hails from Anderson, Indiana. He credits his grandmother with instilling that mentality in him: "She was always one to put everybody before herself. You take care of yourself, you get yourself the bare necessities, but with everything else, you need to help other people. It's really where I learned to stand up for others and to stand up for what's right."

As chairman of Paws' Pantry, Stottlemyer oversaw its move from a tiny, cramped space to a new 1,000-square-foot home in the Campus Center in 2018. He was also instrumental in building the sustainability of Paws' Pantry, which distributed more than 15,000 items during more than 1,300 client visits during the fall semester of 2018.

"As chair of Paws' Pantry, Michael has done an excellent job in his leadership, developing ideas and initiatives focused on growth and sustainability, adaptability, and overall vision for the pantry," said Shaina Lawrence, assistant director for the Office of Student Advocacy and Support.

As second-term president for the Student Activities Programming Board, Stottlemyer was guided by his belief that SAPB programs could create a sense of belonging and community among IUPUI's diverse student population.

Kristin Kreher worked with Michael in her role as a coordinator of student activities in the Campus Center and said, "As president, Michael demonstrated a strong ability to

Facing top Michael Stottlemyer with IUPUI Alumni Council President Leslie Kidwell and Chancellor Paydar at the 2019 Top 100 Undergraduate Recognition Ceremony. *Photo courtesy of IUPUI Alumni Relations.*

Facing bottom From left: Vice Chancellor for Student Affairs Eric Weldy, Director of Student Advocacy and Support Tytishia Davis, Stottlemyer, Assistant Director of Student Advocacy and Support Shaina Lawrence, and Dean of Students Jason Spratt cut the ribbon at the grand reopening of Paws' Pantry. *Photo by Liz Kaye / Indiana University.*

motivate his peers, guide the organization, make decisions, and keep more than eighty members united in their efforts to fulfill the organization's mission."

Under Stottlemyer's leadership, SAPB grew from fewer than thirty active members to more than eighty, allowing the board to increase the number of programs, add a new committee focused on boosting school spirit, add two officer positions for marketing, and engage nearly eleven thousand students in programs, a significant increase over the previous year. Just a few months into his second term, participation in SAPB programs had already tripled compared to previous years.

"Michael is a standout leader with an impressive level of competence, a constant curiosity, a natural ability to build relationships, an understanding of complex systems, and an insistence to challenge the norm," Kreher said. "Through a genuine desire to improve the lives of both friends and strangers alike, he uses his talents, skills, and attitude to leave a lasting impact on the world around him."

Stottlemyer graduated in 2019, but luckily the Hoosier state did not lose his talent. As a recipient of the student scholarship that he lobbied for in 2014, he knows he'll be teaching math to Indiana students for at least five years.

Facing top On May 1, 2019, IUPUI hosted the Lavender Graduation Ceremony to celebrate the achievements of its LGBTQ+ students in the Class of 2019. *Photo by Liz Kaye / Indiana University.*

Facing bottom On May 8, 2019, IUPUI faculty, staff, students, family, and friends gathered to celebrate the graduation of its Class of 2019 Latinx students. *Photo by Liz Kaye / Indiana University.*

SPOTLIGHT ON THE 50TH ANNIVERSARY

A Season for Graduations

Anticipating Our Future:
Jaguars of Tomorrow

Every new class of IUPUI Jaguars brings new possibilities to campus—new creative ideas for how best to teach and how best to learn. Because IUPUI is situated in the heart of Indianapolis, every year also brings new opportunities for partnerships with the city, whether in the form of an internship with the NBA's Indiana Pacers, the mayor's office, or Riley Hospital for Children. Students discover their niche on campus with Jagathon, Paws' Pantry, Regatta, or student government.

The following Faces of IUPUI are current students in 2020 who are finding out what it means to be an IUPUI Jaguar.

Facing top On Saturday, May 11, IUPUI held its 2019 commencement at Lucas Oil Stadium, home of the NFL's Indianapolis Colts. Thousands of family and friends gathered to celebrate the more than seven thousand IUPUI graduates *Photo by James Brosher / Indiana University.*

Facing bottom The Celebration of Black Graduates, a long-standing tradition at IUPUI, was held at the Indiana Convention Center on May 9, 2019. Black graduates from the Class of 2019 gathered with Chancellor Paydar for this group photo prior to the ceremony. *Photo courtesy of GradPhotos.*

Following page top IUPUI students concentrate on a test (undated). *Photo courtesy of IUPUI Special Collections and Archives (UA024–005081s).*

Following page bottom IUPUI student Kathleen Finchum studying in the library in 1986. *Photo courtesy of IUPUI Special Collections and Archives (UA24–005117).*

IUPUI students had to rely on the tried-and-true library card catalog in the age before the internet. *Photo courtesy of IUPUI Special Collections and Archives (UA24–003137n).*

Logan Bromm
IUPUI Class of 2021 (expected), School of Liberal Arts

School of Liberal Arts student Logan Bromm can describe what IUPUI means to him in one word: opportunity. From the beginning, Bromm has been determined to take full advantage of this opportunity because he has never taken higher education for granted.

"I am a first-generation college student. People from my family—even my extended family—do not normally go to college. I constantly remind myself how blessed and lucky I am to have this incredible opportunity. That realization is why I have worked hard to get the most out of my IUPUI experience," said Bromm, a dual major in political science and history from Jasper, Indiana.

Amy Jones Richardson, former assistant director of recruitment, retention, and academic services in the School of Liberal Arts, has witnessed Bromm's fierce determination to thrive during his college years. "When I first met Logan during his freshman orientation, I discovered that he was intent on making the most of every opportunity IUPUI could offer him. As a resident of Honors House, he came to our Liberal Arts Residence Based Learning Community welcome events and proactively introduced himself to fellow students, staff, and administrators. He asked for information about student council and Undergraduate Student Government, scholarships, our honors program, undergraduate research, and networking with alumni. That was the first week. In the two years since then, he has maintained his focus and his academic excellence," she said.

In addition to his outstanding academic achievements, the breadth and depth of his engagement on campus highlight Bromm's commitment to making a difference at IUPUI. As a freshman, he served as vice president of the School of Liberal Arts Student Council and now is its president. He also serves as treasurer of the Honors College Student Council and treasurer of the IUPUI Mock Trial Team. As associate supreme court justice for Undergraduate Student Government, Bromm represents the student body on a variety of advisory committees in addition to helping mediate and settle disputes.

As if this weren't enough, Bromm is also a member of the inaugural Chancellor's Student Advisory Board where he serves with other students as a consistent student voice for Chancellor Nasser H. Paydar and campus leadership. In addition, Bromm is

Facing Logan Bromm. *Photo by Liz Kaye / Indiana University.*

Bromm (top row, far right) with fellow IUPUI campus ambassadors and Jazzy the Jaguar in summer 2018. *Photo courtesy of Logan Bromm.*

a campus ambassador with the Office of Undergraduate Admissions, and his role as a resident assistant in the Office of Housing and Residence Life draws on his natural ability to connect with his fellow students.

"I wanted to make sure that I got the full college experience instead of just going to class and working all the time. Getting involved has been an excellent way for me to network and has allowed me to make both professional contacts and personal friends," said Bromm.

"After I complete my undergrad, I hope to attend law school and discover what area of law I am most passionate about. From there, I simply want to make a meaningful impact for the companies I work for and the communities I live in and serve. My dream has always been to work in government, and being a public servant is an excellent way for me to use my talents to give back to the communities that have made me who I am," he said.

Supriya Chittajallu
IUPUI Class of 2021 (expected), School of Liberal Arts and School of Science

SUPRIYA CHITTAJALLU, A PIKE HIGH SCHOOL graduate and IUPUI student double majoring in biology and medical humanities, had a very busy week in late September 2018. As IUPUI Regatta Arts and Culture Fair coordinator, Chittajallu worked for months with a dedicated student-run steering committee planning the premier canoe race on the Indianapolis Central Canal. Celebrating its tenth anniversary in 2018, Regatta welcomed more than ten thousand people who viewed the race and enjoyed games, entertainment, and other activities.

"I attended Regatta as a freshman, and it was the event that served as my 'aha' moment when I fully accepted that I was a college student at IUPUI. It had been like I was living in a dream up until then, and it was at Regatta that I felt like I officially became a Jaguar," said Chittajallu. "I realized that I wanted to be a part of the group

From left: 2018 IUPUI Regatta Steering Committee members Jason Kabir, Supriya Chittajallu, and Jovana Dodevska chat on the steps of the Indiana State Museum. *Photo by Liz Kaye / Indiana University.*

of students that organizes the event, and when applications opened, I applied to be a member of the steering committee."

Leaders of IUPUI Alumni Relations have been impressed with Chittajallu's work. Andrea Simpson, former assistant vice chancellor and executive director for alumni engagement, said, "In her role as a member of the Regatta steering committee, Supriya has been instrumental in adding a new element to this year's event: the Regatta Arts and Culture Fair. Her efforts in soliciting participation by students, alumni, and others as well as managing all logistic elements of the art fair have helped make this one of the most exciting aspects of the tenth anniversary of Regatta."

Making a splash in Indy's downtown Central Canal, Regatta is more than a highly entertaining canoe race and energetic community festival. It is also a fund-raiser supporting the Stefan S. Davis IUPUI Regatta Scholarship.

"It offers entertainment for everyone and allows the IUPUI and Indianapolis communities to come together for the day to celebrate and benefit the Stefan S. Davis IUPUI Regatta Scholarship. Regatta represents our urban campus, scholarship, and our IUPUI traditions," Chittajallu said.

Chittajallu's campus engagement extends well beyond Regatta. A recipient of the Bepko Scholars and Fellows Program Scholarship, she is also a peer mentor, a member of two honor societies, and, for the last four years, a research intern in the IU School of Medicine's Department of Surgery, a position she started before graduating from high school. After completing her bachelor's degree, she has her sights set on medical school and a future as a physician.

Dr. Steven J. Miller, an associate professor of surgery who has worked with Chittajallu in her role as research intern, said, "She impresses me with her eagerness to learn and her ability to master new techniques. Her enthusiasm is contagious, and she has done an outstanding job not only working in the laboratory but also in communicating her work to scientific and lay audiences. No doubt she will be an excellent physician."

Chittajallu is a Jaguar through and through. "I love IUPUI for its students, staff, and faculty. It has this really amazing heart, and you just feel the love as soon as you walk on campus. I have enjoyed being a part of this campus, and my favorite IUPUI memory is waking up every morning and experiencing it all over again," she said.

Facing Chittajallu sits on the steps of the Indiana State Museum with a view overlooking the city of Indianapolis and the Central Canal where the IUPUI Regatta takes place.
Photo by Liz Kaye / Indiana University.

Will Smith
IUPUI Class of 2020, School of Liberal Arts

IN NEARLY ALL THAT HE DOES, IUPUI STUDENT Will Smith exemplifies what it means to be welcoming and inclusive. As a general studies major with a focus on radiography, Smith is preparing for a career that at its core is about helping people and making them feel comfortable and safe. Smith takes this approach outside the classroom as well in his role as an information specialist and OTEAM leader in the Office of Undergraduate Admissions. He regularly meets and greets prospective students and their families with his infectious smile and upbeat attitude, assisting them along the first part of their IUPUI journey.

Smith's outgoing personality and laid-back demeanor make it easy for students, families, and peers to relate to him. Through his daily interactions, he establishes

Above Will Smith shares a laugh with friends and coworkers from the Office of Admissions. *Photo by Liz Kaye / Indiana University.*

Facing Smith aims for a career where he will be able to connect with and help people. *Photo by Liz Kaye / Indiana University.*

important relationships and creates a positive first impression of IUPUI for future students.

Jen Lund, manager of client services in the Office of Undergraduate Admissions, said of Smith, "What stands out to me about Will is that he is very personable. He is one of the staff members on our team who is always able to welcome students and parents into the office, and he is very outgoing. In this position, you really need to have good customer service skills, and he definitely has them."

The reasons that Smith chose to go to IUPUI are still attractive to him today. "IUPUI is such a diverse community. There is a lot of opportunity here in Indianapolis and so many things you can do. IUPUI has definitely opened my eyes to possibilities and allowed me to grow. It's basically opened me up to becoming a new person," he said.

Though the Gary, Indiana, native graduated in May 2020, he doesn't plan on leaving Indianapolis. He hopes to put his degree to work at Riley Hospital for Children.

Facing top Mayor Hogsett joins IUPUI Jaguars at the 360° Photo Booth, a popular attraction that allowed visitors to create a moving picture memento and post it to social media with the hashtag #MyIUPUI. *Photo by Liz Kaye / Indiana University.*

Facing bottom Chancellor Paydar joined the Student Activities Programming Board to celebrate the great success of Stuff-a-Jag, which SAPB students organized and staffed. All told, a thousand jaguars were stuffed during the IUPUI 50th Anniversary Birthday Bash. *Photo by Liz Kaye / Indiana University.*

Following page Students started dancing the moment the Campus Center doors opened on January 24 and didn't stop until the dance floor was being disassembled. The final song to play, at around 10 p.m., was the IUPUI fight song. *Photo by Liz Kaye / Indiana University.*

Christine Fitzpatrick, director of the IUPUI 50th Anniversary programming and former chief of staff in the Office of the Chancellor, joins Jazzy in cutting the cake during the IUPUI Birthday Bash. *Photo by Liz Kaye / Indiana University.*

EPILOGUE
Olivia Pretorius
IUPUI Jaguar, Class of 2020

VIBRANT MULTICOLORED LIGHTS FADE in and out as students dance in the Campus Center lobby. Towers of cupcakes spill into seeking hands. Upstairs, a line of people winds through the fourth floor as students, faculty, and staff fill plush toy jaguars with soft stuffing. As everyone gathers in the Campus Center to celebrate IUPUI's 50th anniversary with an unforgettable "Birthday Bash," history echoes under their feet.

Beyond the laughter and delight, there's the foundation of a university campus that weaves throughout Indianapolis, with roots of innovation reaching out from under the sidewalks. This is an academic environment that grows with the tide of the city, rising up to learn together. Indianapolis is alive in IUPUI. Since 1969, our school has been dedicated to community engagement, with a mission to serve Indianapolis. IUPUI has been empowering students for fifty years, encouraging creative freedom, supporting free thought, and preparing students to be competent global citizens.

IUPUI has been my home for three years. It's not just a place where I take classes. It is a community of open-minded peers, outstanding professors, and dedicated faculty and staff. I chose to attend IUPUI because our school advocates for diversity and values people for their individuality. Coming from a diverse family of Colombian and South African immigrants made me determined to find a campus that supported cultural awareness, inclusivity, respect, and equality.

At IUPUI, students are valued not only for their intellectual pursuits but also for who they are, where they are from, and what they are passionate about.

Looking at *Fifty Faces and Places of IUPUI*, it is evident that we are a school of diverse innovators, critical thinkers, and international leaders. Each person is strong in their differences. Rather than separating us, diversity on campus connects us in a unique way that allows us to learn from one another and build cultural understanding, challenging ourselves to comprehend new perspectives and drawing us together through excellence in academic dedication.

I have met incredible people at IUPUI, and I'm constantly inspired by my peers. Whether they are returning adult students looking to start a new chapter, first-year freshmen finding their way in the world, or retired veterans building on their passion for knowledge, IUPUI students are tenacious scholars. I am proud to attend IUPUI and to invest in myself through higher education.

Fifty years from now, I envision IUPUI as an urban epicenter of knowledge, a leader in technological advancement, and a powerful catalyst for positive change. I am proud to be an IUPUI Jaguar, and I always will be.

Index

Page numbers in *italics* refer to illustrations.

Cassidy Hunter is Communications Specialist in the Office of the Chancellor at IUPUI. A communications professional for more than two decades, Hunter has experience in marketing, public relations, event planning, and media relations. She has had content published in a variety of print and electronic outlets. She is a member of CASE District V/Great Lakes Region and an IUPUI United Way ambassador.

Becky Wood, Director of Communications in the Office of the Chancellor at IUPUI, has worked as a higher education executive communicator for more than a decade, working at Indiana University, the University of Chicago, and IUPUI. She has presented academic work at dozens of conferences; has a number of publications, including in the *African American Review*; and is also a working visual artist